The ART of
Mentoring

Also by Shirley Peddy

Secrets of the Jungle

The ART of
Mentoring

LEAD, FOLLOW
AND GET OUT
OF THE WAY

SHIRLEY PEDDY, PH.D.

Bullion Books
Houston, Texas

BULLION BOOKS
9597 Jones Rd., 258
Houston, Texas 77065

The organizations and characters in this book are either the product of the author's imagination or a combination of many people and many experiences in many organizations. Any resemblance to a specific company or individual is purely coincidental.

Library of Congress Cataloging-in-Publication

Peddy, Shirley
The Art of Mentoring: Lead, Follow and Get Out of the Way / by Shirley Peddy, Ph.D. 1st edition.
       p.   cm.
       ISBN 0-9651376-3-5
       I. Mentoring in business. 2. Business. 3. Success —
       Psychological Aspects. I. Title.
       DDN 658.3124   HF 5385   LC 98-92757

Book Design by Morgan Printing
Jacket design by Dorothy Wachtenheim

Printed in the United States of America

DEDICATION

To all those who teach, role model, coach, tell stories, explain, listen, counsel, ask the right questions—to a group of one, and to those special mentors who are a continuing source of support and inspiration to me:

> *Jody Heymann*
> *Red Peddy*
> *Donald E. Stanford*
> *George V. Sherman, Jr.*

PREFACE

Most people skip the preface of a book. This introduction is written for those who want to know:

❏ Why mentoring is needed

❏ Why *The Art of Mentoring* is written as a story

❏ Who the book is for

❏ How to use it

One good reason for taking a few minutes to read the preface, and I've made it short, is that it may help you decide if the book is for you or your organization.

Why Mentoring Is Needed

The wave of corporate downsizings of the early nineties was greeted with euphoria by Wall Street and enthusiasm by corporate shareholders. In its wake it has left alienated survivors who no longer count on lifetime employment with one company. While organizations expected that as the inevitable price of terminating large numbers of people, most were convinced that the remaining employees' lost loyalty would be more than compensated by renewing their commitment to learning and personal growth. Career classes were transformed into professional development workshops that exhorted employees to use their jobs to build their résumés and showed them how to manage their own careers. The students listened, and they understood.

Today, just as the demand for knowledge workers is increasing, organizations are helplessly watching the exodus of three-to-five year employees who regard their companies merely as stopping places along their career paths. These former employees have discovered the way to get promotions and higher salaries is to change employers. One three-year employee, who hasn't left *yet*, told me, "I don't know what's wrong. As soon as I get to know people, they are gone. I wonder if I'm making a mistake by staying."

The new employees hired to replace those who leave come from a younger, more diverse group, many of them products of a public education system under siege. (For more on this subject, read Chapter Eleven). They enter organizations on the verge of expansion without the benefit of the mentoring "elders" who departed after taking advantage of lucrative packages offered during the downsizings. Thus, they do their jobs never appreciating the culture and values of the organization they have joined. In time, they too join the exodus. Leaving a company where you do not feel "at home" is easy.

While mentoring cannot be expected to rebuild company loyalty, it can help restore in many employees a sense of connection to their organizations. It should not be assumed that even if a company is aware of its value that mentoring will automatically take place. In some companies, mentors are provided to a select few; in most, mentors are neither encouraged nor honored. Yet corporations, small businesses, universities and volunteer organizations are gradually coming to the realization that you train people in a group, but you *save* them one by one. The purpose of *The Art of Mentoring* is to show those interested how to foster a mentoring culture in which people are respected and rewarded for helping each other succeed.

Why *The Art of Mentoring* Is Written as a Story

In his powerful book *How to Argue and Win Every Time* attorney Gerry Spence writes, "Storytelling has been the principal means by which we have taught one another from the beginning of time." What is mentoring but one person sharing the wisdom of his experience with another? That is one reason it is an art.

People learn in different ways. Some people enjoy stories; others prefer their information in a more structured form. Those who prefer structure may want to focus on the summaries at the end of key chapters. These are called "Notes to Mentoring File" and may be accessed easily through the "Contents." Whatever your choice, I hope you gain practical insights and ideas from reading this book.

Who This Book Is Written For

The Art of Mentoring is for you if you are a manager, human resources professional or a training consultant and your organization is involved in or starting to get involved in mentoring. It applies to small businesses or volunteer organizations as much as it does to large corporations. Any individual who wants to sharpen his skills will find it full of insights and ideas. *Lead, Follow and Get Out of the Way* is meant to be more than a subtitle. It is descriptive of a process that is fully explained in the book.

How to Use It

There are many lessons in the book, and anyone with a job could learn some significant ways to improve just by eavesdropping on the dialogues within. For example, when Rachel teaches Justin how to ask for a raise, she explains to him the three taboos he has violated and gives him examples of what to say and how to say it. There are similar passages regarding handling conflict, transforming a job and making a graceful apology, to name a few.

The Art of Mentoring covers some of the more contentious mentoring issues in organizations today: helping the new employee master the work and unspoken rules, improving interpersonal skills, dealing with job dissatisfaction, *workaholism*, cynicism, and lack of motivation at the end of a career. Training organizations might use it as a casebook. It contains numerous vignettes to illustrate the points covered.

My recommendation is to hand it out to employees as a guidebook and discussion tool while *encouraging* and *rewarding* mentoring. Is mentoring part of what a learning organization does? Of course, but you will see as you read this book, mentoring should not be treated as a program or a workshop. The establishing of a mentoring culture shows the organization's commitment to the employee, and that's why it is a powerful tool that can change the way people think about their work—as well as the companies they work for.

Shirley Peddy
Corpus Christi, Texas
October 1998

CONTENTS

ACKNOWLEDGMENTS

The ideas in this book did not originate with me. Rather they are a culmination of the gifts I have received from many people. It is here that I offer my thanks to those mentoring spirits who have so generously enriched my work.

My sister, Jody Heymann, is one of the people to whom I have dedicated this book. I do not have the space to recite the countless ways she has been a mentor to me, but I want to acknowledge and thank her for the world-class editing she did on this book. Another who has mentored me for twenty-five wonderful years is my husband, Red. How many times can you read one manuscript? He is truly "the wind beneath my wings."

Donald E. Stanford was my major professor and mentor at Louisiana State University. I was going through a very difficult time in my life when I went to Baton Rouge. From him and his gracious wife Marianna, I learned how important it is to mentor the whole person.

I owe a debt of gratitude to George V. Sherman, Jr. for his valuable advice and support on this project as well as on *Secrets of the Jungle*. Using the mentor's art, he has had a positive influence on both books.

Dick Francis, Pat Mulva, Richard Buddeke, Robert Bates, and Larry Kerbow were "silent contributors" to this book. I have watched them give generously of themselves to help others shine more brightly. I owe them my thanks for teaching me the meaning of "the mentoring spirit."

No writer can exist without people willing to read early transcripts and offer their constructive criticism. I have been fortunate to find friends who were willing to share the unfolding of the book with me. Sara Tays and Susan Buddeke provided both advice and moral support as I worked on this project.

In this book I wrote about "mentoring moments," those flashes of insight you receive "on the spot" from someone that help you make a decision or a connection. Sometimes, it is something the person says; sometimes it is something he does. For powerful "mentoring moments" I want to thank Vince Hennessey, Gene Dalton, John Trice, Roberta Wood-Hughes, Merida Steele, Dave Radcliffe, and Dianne Burns.

Finally, I am grateful to my daughters Dana Beard and Terri Pitts and their husbands, Jon Beard and Martin Pitts, for showing me how to handle life's obstacles with a mixture of humor and perseverance. I also want to thank them for the many stories they have shared about life at work.

One of the things mentors do is to pass down their wisdom through such stories. Three of the most delightful storytellers I've ever learned from are Dr. Hans Heymann, Polly Kerbow, and Geri Sherman. May they sit around the campfire forever, teaching us what we need to know about life.

Storytelling has been the principal means by which we have taught one another from the beginning of time. The campfire. The tribal members gathered round, the little children peeping from behind the adults, their eyes as wide as dollars, listening, listening. The old man—can you hear his crackly voice, telling his stories of days gone by? Something is learned from the story—the way to surround and kill a saber-toothed tiger, the hunt for the king of the mastodons in a far-off valley, how the old man survived the storm. There are stories of love, of the discovery of magic potions, of the evil of the warring neighboring tribes—all learning of man has been handed down for eons in the form of stories.

Gerry Spence

How to Argue and Win Every Time

To the Reader

My name is Rachel Hanson, and I'm going to tell you a tale not of two cities but of two companies. One of these companies, To Your Health, Inc. (TYH), makes and sells vitamins, herbal remedies, and other health products, which are produced at its plant in Sugar Land, Texas, and marketed through its sales office in Houston. The other is my employer, Perry Winkle Enterprises (PWE), a conglomerate with its main focus on the food, home chemicals, and pharmaceutical industries. Where the history of these two companies intersected is but a backdrop for my real story, which is about people like you and me who are committed to helping others succeed by passing down the important lessons we've learned. I want to share this with you because of a letter I received yesterday. I am still captured by its messages, and I want to reveal those messages within the context of my story because it's important to me that you understand.

PROLOGUE:
THE CHALLENGE

In 1995, Perry Winkle Enterprises acquired TYH, leaving its management intact. By March of 1996, PWE's management was concerned about TYH's own "long range health" and was wondering, behind closed doors, whether the acquisition had been a mistake. In spite of the national focus on fitness, sales had been slipping, and what at first had appeared a blip on the balance sheet was beginning to look like a trend. The following month a new marketing manager, one with PWE credentials, was installed, the former manager having taken advantage of a generous benefits package and exited stage right.

Ben Turner put in four months, had a massive heart attack, and took an early retirement from PWE. Then, to make matters worse, two weeks later To Your Health's Wholesale Marketing Supervisor left for greener pastures. Things were in disarray. That's when I entered the scene. I'm a former marketer turned organizational effectiveness consultant, and I work for the Pharmaceutical Division of Perry Winkle. The project I had been involved in was near completion, and Elroy Grant, our Vice President (a.k.a. "the drug czar of PWE"), asked Ira Sharp, Human Resources Manager, to loan me to him as a temporary candidate to fill in as Wholesale Marketing Supervisor while a permanent and available replacement could be identified. Ira agreed, and Elroy sent for me.

There were few at PWE who did not know Elroy, and fewer still who can say "no" to him. He looks like a grizzly bear and sounds like a lion. His roaring voice and hearty laugh echo up and down the eleventh floor where PWE management resides. He is cheerleader, devil's advocate, mentor, and hard-liner, all at once. If you want to see him, you have to be fast on your feet because he might be roaming the halls on any floor, walking into offices, engaging people in conversation, and finding out what is on their minds.

You can get into interesting debates with Elroy. They are hard to win not only because of his position, although that helps, but also because he has a very keen mind. I had learned that the best way to get along with him is to challenge his thinking, but you'd better be right or at least very convincing. You either love him or hate him. I belong in the former group, having worked for him six years before and with him a number of times since as an internal consultant.

Sitting across from his huge desk and leather chair, I felt dwarfed by him. I'm 5'4", so I looked up to him in more ways than one. "I need you at TYH," he told me, "but it's going to be a challenge, Rachel." He held up three fingers of his left hand. "In the first place," he said, using his right index finger to bend the left one back, "don't be surprised if the TYHers aren't thrilled with another boss from PWE. In the second place," he said bending back the next finger, "the fact that you're temporary, and they know it, means they'll see you as a surrogate. That's something like a substitute teacher, without the respect. Finally, you're going to know something they don't know," he said, tapping on the third finger, "and that'll have an impact on you. You see, part of your job will be to assess the sales staff and recommend who should stay and who should be reassigned or terminated. I don't need to tell you, your recommendation will carry a lot of weight with me."

"Why pick me for this?" I asked. "I'm not in management. I don't see myself as The Terminator, and besides my work is to help organizations be more effective."

"Because I know how good you are at assessing situations. Besides that, I've seen you work with people, and I trust you. It's a bit of a test, Rachel. As a contributor, you shine. As a coach, you're top-notch. I'm wondering if you can make the tough calls."

"Just a minute, Elroy," I said, "suppose no one should be fired? What if the problems are with the processes and not the people? I don't want to go to TYH as a PWE hatchet man (or woman)." I knew Elroy long enough and well enough to challenge him—especially when it involved a matter of principle.

"Fair enough," he grinned. When he smiles like that, he looks like James Earl Jones, a black actor I admire greatly. "If anyone can pull this off, you can. At the very least, you'll get material for the mentoring course you've been wanting to put on. Just don't forget, Rachel, things have to change. If there's someone there who doesn't get the message, if they don't reverse the downward trend, then...." He drew his index finger across his neck. I got the message. So, it was agreed. I would move to Houston temporarily, but the assignment probably wouldn't last more than two to three months. I promised to stay in touch with Elroy by e-mail as well as to talk to him regularly about our progress.

That was the beginning of my adventure.

CHAPTER 1

Mentors and Mentoring

> *By themselves, character and integrity do not accomplish anything. But their absence faults everything else.*
>
> — Peter Drucker

L ooking back, I am no longer puzzled by Elroy's choice. He knew full well I could not supervise the marketers. I knew far too little about their business to help them sell more products. I had spent much of my career learning about what makes people successful. In this, I had been teacher, adviser and supporter to many at PWE. Those were the roles I played best, and Elroy knew it. He remembered what I had said to him about the mentoring course. Maybe that was why he

23

chose me. To Your Health presented a challenge for me, and it was the learning opportunity that drew me there.

When I think about being a mentor, I recall the story of the starfish. A beachcomber is walking along the beach one morning when he sees a young man running up and down by the water's edge throwing something in the water. Curious, he walks toward the runner and watches him picking up starfish stranded by the tide and tossing them back into the ocean. "Young man," he says, "there are so many starfish on the beach. What difference does it make to save a few?"

Without pausing, the young man picks up another starfish, and flinging it into the sea, replies, "It made a difference for this one." That's what mentors do. They make a difference for one person at a time. That is why I am telling you my story. I want to make a difference for you, and I'm hoping you in turn will decide to do the same for someone else.

What Is a Mentor?

The word originated from Greek mythology. Mentor was the name of a wise and faithful advisor to Odysseus. When Odysseus (or Ulysses as the Romans called him) left for his long voyage, he entrusted the direction and teaching of his son Telemachus to Mentor. According to mythology, through Mentor's guidance Telemachus became an effective and loved ruler. Today, the word is most often used to mean a friend and role model, an able advisor, a person who lends support in many different ways to one pursuing specific goals.

Why Mentoring Is an Art

Mentoring is not a science. People have different goals and come from different life experiences. One who would mentor must be able to determine the best help to offer. Some who seek advice have no idea what the right questions are; others, mistakenly or correctly, believe they know the answers and are merely seeking confirmation. Both represent a challenge. Sometimes the mentor must be a story teller; at other times, an empathetic listener. Occasionally, it's a coach's *pep talk* that is needed. The art is not merely knowing *what* to say but *how* to say it and *when*.

Some information one would share with others is delicate. I know a manager who helped a woman succeed by recommending an image makeover. He recognized her ability to move ahead, but he knew she didn't look like a manager. Should that matter? Probably not, but it does. So he took a risk, and with the mentor's art, he was able to frame his suggestion in such a way that she understood the good intentions behind it. There's no cookbook for mentoring, but there is a process that works.

How Mentors Do It

The process of mentoring can best be described in eight words: *lead, follow and get out of the way*! I learned that from a very wise man, but I'll tell you more about that later. For now, the important thing is to understand the mentoring process. I think of *leading* as showing the way by role modeling, experience, or example; *following*, as advising and counseling (when asked) and *getting out of the way* as the art of withdrawing from a supportive relationship, while leaving the door open for a more collegial one.

Sounds simple, doesn't it? Yet, there are some complex points we need to consider. First of all, the process works differently when the person you want to mentor is a young adult, an ambitious new hire, a thirty-something workaholic, a cynical baby boomer or a fifty-year-old coasting toward the final five. I am going to share what I learned about these differences.

Second, the process is not necessarily linear. Sometimes mentors move back and forth between leading and following. People need space to experiment and even to make mistakes.

Sometimes "getting out of the way" isn't all that easy, or it may be desirable for one party but not the other. Most people don't want to hear your problems, but almost everyone loves to give advice. One of the pitfalls of helping another is becoming over-invested in that advice or wanting to be in control. In spite of all this, I've always found mentoring very rewarding.

But let me get back to my story. It was 1996, and I was getting ready for my two to three months in Houston.

Can You Mentor Your Own Children?

I remember the mixed feelings I had about moving to Houston. On one hand, it seemed like a fascinating challenge. On the other, it meant leaving my husband Paul to "bach" it. We live in the quiet village of Oakville, Georgia, home of PWE's Pharmaceutical Division. That's a long way from the bustling city of Houston, culturally and emotionally.

Paul would have an extra challenge. Along with his home building business, he would be entrusted with the "care and feeding" of our nineteen-year-old son Brad, who had just dropped out after one mediocre year of college. He had been spending the last two months at home "rethinking" his life, and I got the impression Paul wanted him to accelerate that process, meaning get a job or go back to school, which increased my concern about leaving. Paul had assured me all would be well. I believed Brad needed someone to talk to who could point him in the right direction, and based on the results we had already experienced, that person wasn't Paul or me. For this reason, I don't recommend mentoring your own children. When they are in your care, when you are responsible for their well being and deeply involved in their decisions, then what you do is called *parenting*. Your advice always has an emotional twist to it. There's an innate desire on their part to please or, in Brad's case, to rebel.

The mentoring relationship may have some of these components, but it doesn't have the intense "push and pull" quality of parenting. Does that still hold when children get older? I think it does. Still, the parent, like the mentor is a role model. The results of this aspect of parenting show up in the choices young adults make and how they treat others. Are their relationships compassionate and caring or needy and controlling? Are they willing to accept the consequences of their decisions, or do they prefer to stay at home and hold on to their childhood? In Brad's case, the jury was still out.

Mentoring Requires Objectivity and Distance

Let me give you an example. A young man I knew was having some difficulties at work. Dave transferred into a different job, and his new supervisor made premature judgments about him based on one or two missed deadlines. There were reasons Dave had missed them, for he had not been given the information he needed. His supervisor had delegated Dave's training to a co-worker, who was buried under his own work and not the least bit interested in training someone he regarded as competition for top ranking.

Dave's performance was suffering. Repeated attempts to discuss this situation with his supervisor led to little more than frustration. Now, Dave was single and an only child with understandably concerned parents. His father rushed to his rescue. He was totally on Dave's side, characterizing the supervisor as a bully and pushing Dave to report him to the manager. Phil had the best intentions but no experience with corporate culture since he owned a small coin shop, which he had inherited from his father. As an advocate for his son, his approach to Dave's problem, while well-intentioned, was far too parochial.

Fortunately, Dave had a former supervisor who understood how things work within the company. Gene's advice to Dave was to focus his energy on improving his performance, not on impressing his supervisor. Gene knew Dave's supervisor to be somewhat unapproachable. He also knew that by working more diligently to satisfy customers, Dave would have the best opportunity to influence his supervisor's perception. *Nothing, Gene assured Dave, would give him more credit than good reports from others.*

Gene's insight and perspective were what Dave needed to solve his problem. He took the advice and, in time, just as Gene predicted, word of his efforts and the results filtered back to his supervisor with a positive effect. That brings me to the next question.

Should Supervisors Mentor Subordinates?

I've asked a number of people this question. Their responses are mixed. Some were mentored by supervisors or managers but only *after* they left the groups they were in. Some have never had a mentor. Only one was mentored by his supervisor, but they had a special bond from the beginning based on a common hobby.

The real issue is the same as with parenting. Parents have a responsibility for their children. *Supervisors are primarily responsible for the group's performance.* That means the welfare of the whole is above the immediate needs of the individual. If a supervisor chooses to mentor an individual, that could create a conflict of interests, first by her preferring one employee over another and second, by her subordinating the team's needs to that of the individual. Good supervisors don't do either. There is a certain amount of distance from the every day "battlefield" required in a mentoring situation, and supervisors, by definition, are in the midst of the action. So my recommendation to supervisors is be a coach, be a supporter, and give performance advice to the people who report to you. Those are all part of the supervisory relationship, or should be, but leave mentoring to someone else. My advice to people looking for mentors is pick someone away from the field of battle.

What Do Mentors Do?

A mentor is teacher, coach, sponsor, counselor, advisor—to a group of one. Her interest is in you as an individual. Mentors teach you the unspoken rules of an organization: how to dress, what to say, how to get projects approved, insider information that can make or break a career. Sometimes they pass on information not generally known or warn you about particular pitfalls. They keep you from wearing a brown suit when a blue or gray one is required or responding to the wrong question in a meeting. They make introductory phone calls and lend you support in countless other ways. They share their experiences with you, the ones they won't tell anyone else, and they expect something back for that: loyalty, confidentiality, attention, appreciation and commitment to a common goal. Some mentors do all of these things; some, just one or two. Sometimes one happens to find a mentor in a former supervisor or manager. Sometimes, if you're lucky, a mentor finds you.

Organizations know their value. That's why they establish mentoring programs to "jump start" new employees or help longer-service ones overcome obstacles. These are worthwhile efforts; however, their success varies *because it is based on the dedication of those who participate.* Assigned mentors are like arranged marriages; some take, some don't. It all depends on commitment and chemistry. The ideal situation is when two individuals form a common bond. Then, stand back and watch what happens!

I've been fortunate to form those bonds with several people. That's why, in spite of my marching orders from Elroy, I decided to focus not on the group, not on their performance, but on each of the marketers as individuals. I had been assured a supervisor would soon be along. In the meantime, my intention was to be a mentor to each of them.

CHAPTER 2

First Impressions

*Authority without wisdom is like a heavy axe without
an edge, fitter to bruise than polish.*

— Anne Bradstreet

T wo years have passed since I returned from my
adventure in Houston. Yet, every once in a while,
something unexpected brings back vivid memories of
the past. That's what happened yesterday. When I arrived home
from work, I found a note from Paul on the refrigerator. He had
a meeting with a client which included dinner. He sent his love
and said he would see me about nine. There was a letter
postmarked Houston lying on the counter. It began:

Dear Rachel,
*I'll bet you're surprised to receive this a couple of years after
your brief stay at TYH. I was with a group of friends last night*

having dinner at Oscar's, and we got to talking about you. Do
you remember what things were like when you came here?

Two Years Earlier: Houston

As I read those words, my thoughts went back to a rainy September day two years ago. It was my fourth day in Houston, and I was sitting at the top of the landing in the two-story apartment complex where I would live for the next few months. It was nothing like home but temporarily passable. Arrangements had been made over the phone. My new home was in one of those brick buildings with four or five dozen units surrounding two swimming pools. I had received a security card, and when I drove through the iron gates and they slowly closed behind me, I knew I was in the big city. But, here I was sopping wet on the landing, a small bag of dripping groceries beside me, my purse open, its contents sprawled out next to me, and searching frantically for my door key.

I had arrived on Friday and spent the day moving in. This was Monday, my first day at the office, and I wondered if I had left it on my desk. I heard a cough and, looking to my left, saw two brown oxfords beside me. "I hope I didn't startle you," said my neighbor Elizabeth Powell, a slim gray-haired woman I had met briefly when I was moving in. "I was wondering if I could help."

I looked up. Frankly, I was glad to see a friendly face. Things had been pretty frosty my first day at TYH. In fact, the only friendly face I had seen the whole day belonged to Judy Simpson, the temporary secretary brought in to assist me. We were in the same boat. No one knew, or cared to know, either of us. When I went around to introduce myself, people were polite but not very welcoming. Who could blame them? Another temporary replacement from PWE had arrived on the scene. I was an outsider just as Elroy had predicted. It was up to me to prove myself. I knew I would, but at the moment "how" escaped me.

31

Elizabeth picked up the milk and frozen orange juice. "I'll just put these in my refrigerator so they don't spoil, "she said, shaking the water off of them. "You need a towel, my dear." She invited me for tea promising to call the manager or maintenance, who, she assured me, would bring a key right up. I replaced the contents in my purse and followed her across the hall. As we entered the apartment, I heard a husky male voice from another room. "That you, Lizzy?" "It's just Lucien," said Elizabeth. "He's surfing the net, but I refuse to answer when he calls me Lizzy. He knows I hate that."

As Elizabeth poured two steaming cups of tea, she told me that Lucien was searching for background data for a paper he was writing about culture and values in today's business world. He had retired two years before and had published several articles about business since then. The Powells had recently sold their home and were looking for a smaller one. In the meantime, they were transients, like me. I told Elizabeth, who asked me to call her Beth, that I had been sent to Houston by Perry Winkle Enterprises to replace the recently departed wholesale marketing supervisor for To Your Health. I was concerned that I might be walking into a nest of swarming hornets. Sales had fallen and, according to the former Marketing Manager Ben Turner, the staff weren't happy at all. There were even undertones that people might be looking elsewhere for jobs. Beth provided a sympathetic ear, and I was thankful for that. At the moment, a good listener was exactly what I needed.

Meanwhile, lured by the smell of freshly-baked oatmeal cookies, Lucien joined us. He was a tall slender man in his sixties, with more sandy hair than most men half his age. He entered the conversation briefly—long enough for me to learn that he had spent the last ten years of his career at TYH. "It's probably a different world than you're used to," he told me. His words, "If I might make a suggestion," were interrupted by a knock on the door. It was the manager, master-key in hand. Thanking Beth for the cookies and tea, I departed. Lucien looked disappointed.

"Come back any time," he told me. I knew I would, but at that moment, I had no idea how often it would be.

When I returned to my apartment that night, I found the missing key on the night stand beside my bed. On the small desk in my bedroom was my laptop computer. Before I went to bed, I sent a brief message to Elroy.

```
To: egrant@pwe.net
From: rachel@pwe.net
```

TYH seems like such a cold place. Where are the free spirits you might expect to see in a company that is dedicated to health? The walls are painted white, and there are a precious few pictures scattered here and there. The offices I passed today were all but devoid of decorations. It was almost as if everything and everyone was temporary, and someone had cleaned up the place to be ready for the next tenant.

And it's too quiet for me—a far cry from the noisy energy of Perry Winkle Enterprises. People stay in their offices and mostly seem to speak in whispers. Thank goodness the place is carpeted. If not, I might have been spooked by the echo of my footsteps as I walked down the hall.

Tomorrow, as pre-arranged by you, I am to meet the President, Altis Dunlop, for lunch. I also plan to introduce myself to the marketing group. Judy, my temporary assistant, is arranging a meeting for 3 p.m. I wonder what they will be like and how they will react to one more person parachuting in from Perry Winkle Enterprises. Stay tuned.

Rachel

* * *

Tuesday morning began with the arduous tasks of moving in. The four boxes I had packed so carefully before leaving PWE stood sentinel beside my desk. They did nothing to harm the décor of my office. My temporary quarters had the look of a room in an inexpensive motel. I made a mental note: if I were going to make it through the next three months, I'd need to do something to warm it up.

Just then, Judy walked in to report on the status of today's meeting. A tall, slim middle-aged woman, she had an air of competence and the warmest smile I had seen at To Your Health. Four of the marketers had indicated they were coming—a little reluctantly, she reported. The fifth had offered her apologies. Gayle was sick with a stomach virus and would be out today and possibly tomorrow. Judy handed me the personnel files I had requested earlier. I decided to read through them before the meeting, but I would skim the performance appraisals, preferring to make my own assessments. Judy lingered long enough to give me some bad news. She was looking for a permanent job and would probably be leaving in two weeks. She asked, and received, permission to do some interviewing. I made a mental note to call HR. I liked Judy, and I wondered if there were some chance TYH could make her an offer. Then I returned to the folders. I was in the midst of them when the phone rang. It was Judy. "I just wanted to remind you of your lunch appointment," she said.

Management at TYH

Lunch with Altis Dunlop, President of TYH, was not at all what I expected. He seemed a man suspended in time and space. He let me know he was not sure he would be staying since he had been offered a separation package by PWE and had been given three months to make a decision. That was over a month ago. We talked about many things, but nothing of substance. Looking back, I realize it was little more than a courtesy meeting. Altis was a man in his late fifties. His thinning hair and high-pitched voice made him seem much older. He had been president of TYH for five years, moving up from Vice President to President shortly before Griff Lawrence, then CEO, retired. Now he was considering the separation offer, but he told me he was also waiting to see what, if any, other opportunities PWE might present.

Based on early impressions and my long association with PWE, I could have told him not to hold his breath. When PWE offers a manager the opportunity to make a graceful exit, there's little more to say than *yes*. Should you choose to remain, the next step is generally corporate oblivion, with your new (and much smaller) desk moved to some forgotten corner, a secretary that visits on alternate Fridays and an obscure administrative project that no one bothers to ask about because no one really cares.

During lunch, Altis expressed concern about Ben Turner saying he hoped the marketing job hadn't been responsible for his heart trouble. I hoped so too. He wished me luck and told me if he could help, give him a call. That was it. Any attempts I made to get his perspective on why marketing was in the doldrums were met with vague comments like, "I think the people in Marketing might want to help you with that." Altis suggested I talk with Charlie Rothstein, the previous head of Marketing, who was now managing the plant in Sugar Land. He said Charlie had been with TYH for over twenty years and knew "where all the bodies were buried."

The Marketers

So, I was back on my own and looking forward to meeting the marketers with a mixture of curiosity and anxiety. In retrospect, I think they knew that as yesterday's letter points out.

I'll bet you weren't exactly thrilled with our first meeting: one missing, one late, and all of us acting like we were part of a command performance at the home of a spinster aunt.

I laugh as I think about that comment. It is only too accurate. The meeting was scheduled for three. First to arrive was Alicia Juarez. A small, slim woman, she was carrying a folder, a pen and a steno pad in one hand and a can of soda in the other. Almost from the moment she entered the room, Alicia seemed uncomfortable, fidgeting with her pen, tapping on the soda can and responding to my friendly inquiries with all the spontaneity of a contestant picking letters for Wheel of Fortune.

Alicia processed all the orders, and dealt with customer complaints. She was thirty-five and had worked in the sales office of TYH for six years. According to her file, she was a hard worker, arriving at seven each morning. Ben had expressed concern because she stayed every afternoon until 5:30 or later, rarely leaving her office and eating lunch at her desk. She had a degree in Business Administration, and I was puzzled that she was in a support staff position. A previous supervisor had noted that Alicia had been offered, and had rejected, a better paying sales position He didn't say why, but I resolved to find out more.

Stuart Kennedy and Katy Jackson walked in together: I had heard them laughing and talking as they neared my office, but when they entered the door, they were silent and solemn. I introduced myself, and Stuart smiled as he shook my hand. Did I feel a slight pressure in the joints of my fingers, or was that my imagination? A slim athletic-looking man in his early forties, Stuart was of medium height, blond and slightly graying. It was his expression that caught me off guard. Was his smile patronizing and a bit sardonic, or was I just reacting to some of the "press releases" in his personnel file? Ben had described him as cynical and disgruntled. The manager before Ben had found him argumentative. His file suggested that Stuart had been a real go-getter at TYH, at one time slated for company management. I wondered if he had gotten caught in the flattening of the organization or had been moved aside because of his attitude. Perhaps these two factors were linked, and he was disappointed that his career at TYH hadn't taken the direction he wanted. Either way, I resolved to keep an open mind.

I turned toward Katy, extending my hand. A tall athletic black woman, she looked like a poster girl for health products. As she shook my outstretched hand, I had the feeling she was sizing me up. The feeling was mutual. Katy's file was filled with glowing recommendations from her former professors at Stanford. A relatively new hire, she was twenty-three and had been with To Your Health for about seven months. She had come to TYH in the midst of crisis with the company on a down curve and constant changes in management. Until now, she had not lived up to Marketing's high expectations of her. I wondered if she had received the help she needed to succeed.

The four of us engaged in the usual small talk. How was my trip? Was I finding everything I needed? How did I like Houston? To Your Health was a little company, a big change from Perry Winkle Enterprises, wasn't it? I asked them questions I already knew the answer to. How long have you been here? What are you doing now? All efforts to fill the time as we waited for the last member of our group, Tom Gaines. I looked at my watch. He was now ten minutes late. We were not off to an auspicious beginning. The file on Tom Gaines had been enlightening, to say the least. He was the quintessential salesman—the man everyone liked. That didn't include me, at least not right now.

"Where's Gayle," Alicia asked, waking me from my reverie.

"I understand she has a virus," I responded.

I remember the way Stuart and Katy looked at each other, then quickly back at me. "Yes," said Stuart. "I hear it's going around." Katy giggled.

I decided to ignore what was going on, making a mental note to ask Judy what she knew about Gayle.

I remember how I felt when Tom finally showed up, twenty minutes late and with Charlie Rothstein in tow. A stocky man with a thick neck and a big smile, he put out a large, fleshy hand. "Hi, Rachel," he said, as if he'd known me for years. "Meet Charlie Rothstein, the sugar man from Sugar Land." I smiled and put out my hand. Frankly, I was annoyed, but I remembered something Elroy had said to me many years ago. There had been angry words in a meeting, and some of them were mine. After the meeting, he had come to my office, sat down and looking me straight in the eye said, "This isn't personal, Rachel. It's business. Get emotional and you've lost."

"But, they finally saw it my way," I had said, not a little defensively.

"Did they? They may have conceded, but they will remember how you reacted. Word gets around. Next time, people may come at you from a more adversarial position. Take it from somebody who's been there. You have to pick your battles. Remember, *negotiation is more rewarding than confrontation*. It's also more lasting."

With Tom Gaines, I recognized a no-win situation immediately. First, I knew I was being tested—and in front of a very important audience. I had a position of authority, and that made me doubly careful about using it. The group would take my measure based on how I responded, so rather than be heavy-handed, I decided to greet Charlie and Tom as if nothing had happened and wait until later to find out why Tom was late.

Charlie said he had to go. I thanked him for coming by and said I'd like to meet with him as soon as it was convenient. He left, promising to call me in the morning. From what I had been told by Altis Dunlop, Charlie Rothstein would make a powerful ally. I decided to do my best to make that happen.

As for Tom, I waited until the meeting was over and asked him to stay for just a moment. He knew why. The minute the others left, he apologized for being late. "I was on the phone with a customer," he told me. I nodded my understanding, and he was gone. We had both played "the game." I had forced him to explain, and, of course, he came up with the answer I could not refute. The discussion had neither helped, nor hurt, but it allowed both of us to save face.

What about the meeting? I had originally planned to ask the marketers to help me understand what was happening at TYH. After the first few minutes, I realized they were being evasive and that no questions I asked stood the slightest chance of being answered, so I used the time to get acquainted.

From my perception, we were off to a rocky start. After twenty minutes of introductions, I promised to visit with each of them individually in the next few days and asked that they spend some time thinking about what they might want to discuss. Then the meeting was over, except for my short discussion with Tom.

My second full day at TYH had given me much to think about. Before leaving for the apartment, I sent a quick e-mail note to Elroy.

```
To: egrant@pwe.net
From: rachel@pwe.net

    Lunch with President: formal. Meeting with
    Marketers: more formal. Short tour of
    building: most formal. TYH needs to loosen
    up. Talk to you later.

    Rachel
```

When I got back to my apartment, there was a computer note taped to the door. "Come to dinner. We're having chicken and dumplings. No excuses. Beth is the world's greatest cook." It was signed Lucien Powell. Underneath those words, was a handwritten postscript. "Dinner is at 7. Please come. Beth"

After a delicious dinner, and at her insistence, Lucien and I had sat in two comfortable rockers while Beth cleaned up the dishes. "In this postage stamp kitchen, you'll only be in the way," she had said of my offers to help. "You go keep Lucky company. I won't be long."

"Is coffee on the way?" Lucien had asked.

"You know it is," said Beth.

"Is Lucky your nickname?" I asked.

"Only to Lizzy," he replied.

I smiled. They were truly a warm and affectionate couple, and I hoped to introduce Paul when and if he could pay a visit to Houston. "What can you tell me about TYH?" I asked Lucien, knowing it had been only two years since he retired.

"Which TYH are you interested in? The one we had ten years ago, five years ago, or when I left?" he asked me. "The headquarters TYH or the plant in Sugar Land?" he continued.

Apparently the company had made several key changes. My dilemma was I didn't know which one to ask about. So I responded, "All the above." That evening, I began to understand some things about TYH.

Morale at To Your Health, Lucien's Story

Lucien had been the Distribution Manager and finally Plant Manager in Sugar Land. Headquarters had always been a bit buttoned-down and stuffy, he told me; however, the general attitude was TYHers were a family, and the company cared about each individual employee. People enjoyed working there. Business was great. There was a young, energetic, and optimistic quality to the sales force. "We had carved out a niche for ourselves," he said. "It was high quality, and our labs operated closely in conjunction with the plant.

"Unfortunately, nothing stays the same," he continued. "Our business was challenged by a more global economy, and the same forces that brought about changes in other places began to affect us. The health products market got very competitive, particularly in regard to price. A problematic cycle began. Forgetting our quality niche, there was a push by management to lower costs, which was soon followed by a determination that what cost the company the most was employees. Sound familiar? So we had our first 'incentive to leave' program. People looked around and said, 'Is this my family? I don't think so.' Some left gladly; others were forced out. Prices were lowered. One who left was our President, Griff Lawrence. He was almost like a father to a whole lot of people, having been president for over fifteen years. The man who replaced him was Altis Dunlop."

Lucien told me that Altis had been chief financial officer for years, and people felt that he was instrumental in forcing Lawrence out. Now he was being rewarded for it. That didn't sit well. No one was saying that Griff Lawrence was perfect, but he was loved and respected. After the downsizing, people didn't feel quite as committed, partly because of the change in management, but mostly because they felt the company had broken faith with them.

"Other companies have downsized and done very well afterwards," I remember telling Lucien, thinking particularly of my company, Perry Winkle Enterprises.

"It's how things are handled," he responded. "You've got to help people *through* a massive change. Altis didn't know that, and when others told him, he looked back at the only authority he respected—the books, and refused to listen."

"So then what?" I had asked.

"So then, things returned to normal for a while, but productivity was not quite as high. Altis looked at the numbers the following quarter, and he brought his managers in. 'This is not acceptable,' he told us. 'Find more ways to cut costs.'"

"Did he consider working 'the other side of the street?'" I asked. "Maybe, expand sales, increase quality even more, introduce a new product or product line?"

"All those things were suggested. His response was, "Do them all *and* cut costs."

"Is that why TYH was put on the market?" I wondered.

"It didn't happen right away, but that was the inevitable outcome," Lucien had told me. He wasn't sure how that had come about, only that in a down cycle, being acquired by a company far away with a management no one knew anything about did not turn out to be a big motivator.

Beth arrived with the coffee, the kitchen having been put to rights, and the conversation moved to me, my family, and my feelings about leaving them for several months. I told them I was lonesome. I spoke of Paul and his work and about Brad, who had decided to "sit the world out" for several months. Beth was sympathetic, but Lucien seemed to feel that his time alone with Paul might possibly produce a more responsible attitude. I wasn't so sure.

Looking at my watch, I saw it was after nine. Five o'clock would come no matter how much or how little sleep I got, so I thanked the Powells and returned to my small apartment across the hall. That night I dreamed of spider webs and white painted walls.

CHAPTER 3

Developing Relationships

*Have respect for every person and every issue directed
at you. Do not dismiss any encounter as insignificant.*

— John Heider *The Tao of Leadership*

T he morning commute to downtown Houston depends
on how early you are willing to get out of bed. From
where I was staying, if I left my apartment between 6:15
and 6:30, it usually took twenty minutes. Any later, and I was
looking at thirty to forty minutes, depending on the weather
and also on how skillfully Houston drivers were avoiding each
other that day. An accident, no matter which side of the freeway,
could add another ten to twenty minutes, based on how serious
it was and how quickly the wreckers arrived. So, I had plenty of

time as I drove to work the next morning in my TYH pool car to plan my day.

My strategy wasn't very complex. Since the marketers didn't seem very forthcoming in a group, I decided to visit with each of them individually, starting with whoever was there. I also needed to talk with Judy. Perhaps she could explain the situation with Gayle that had precipitated those sidelong looks between Stu and Katy when her name was mentioned.

My first act, however, was to check my e-mail. I figured I'd hear from Elroy, and I was right.

```
From: egrant@pwe.net
To: rachel@pwe.net

    TYH may be formal, but they've met their
    match in you. One word of advice, the first
    and foremost job of a leader is to recruit.
    Good luck.

    Elroy
```

All right, I thought. So Elroy knows I can't lead without followers. Easier said than done, I sighed. He was right. It was time to start. As I picked up my empty coffee cup and headed for the door, I was intercepted by Judy. Charlie Rothstein was in the building and had stopped by her desk. I had an invitation to lunch, but Judy could page him if I couldn't make it. Otherwise, he'd stop by and pick me up at 11:30. I told her I'd be ready and asked her if she had seen Alicia. She pointed toward the coffee room. "She's either in there or squirreled behind her door," Judy replied. It's 4-C, right across from the coffee room."

"Before I go," I asked her, "have you heard anything from Gayle? How is she?"

"I really don't know, but I'll call her," answered Judy. "By the time you get back, I should know something."

I headed straight for the coffee room. Moments later I was

standing in the doorway of Alicia's office. I wasn't sure if it was tiny or appeared smaller than it was because of the massive metal desk that seemed to fill the room. On top of the desk were numerous stacks of paper piled high and neatly arranged. A computer sat on a small table perpendicular to the desk. Behind the desk was a credenza heaped high with notebooks. I sat down in the straight-backed visitor's chair to the right of the desk after removing several three-ring binders from it. Alicia was talking on the phone, which was perched on her shoulder. Occasionally she asked a question, keying in the response on her computer. Up until this point, she hadn't acknowledged my presence in any way. I decided to wait.

The door opened wider and Tom Gaines rushed in, dropped some papers into the box marked "in," which rested on the left-hand corner of her desk, waved to Alicia, nodded to me and was gone before I had a chance to speak. About that time, Alicia completed her call and turned to me with a weak smile.

"Can I get you some coffee or a soda?" I asked. Looking at me quizzically, Alicia produced a large blue mug hidden behind one stack. "I thought we might get better acquainted," I said, more heartily than I felt. The phone rang, and Alicia looked at it and back at me like a trapped rabbit. "Do you have call notes?" I asked. She nodded. "Maybe we could talk in the small conference room across from my office." She hesitated and then picking up her cup walked toward the door. Up until now, she hadn't said a word. I could tell this discussion wasn't going to be easy.

Building Trust

Many years before, I had learned a three-step strategy that helps to "prime the pump" of conversation. First, you look for common ground, something you share with the other person, no matter how small. Second, you begin building trust by revealing something about yourself. Finally, you ask open-ended, non-loaded questions to increase the other person's comfort level. On the way to the conference room, I decided I'd better use this process, or Alicia and I would probably have the shortest discussion on record. This is how the process works:

Find Common Ground: It may be the weather, the traffic or something in the morning news—on any given day, we share dozens of experiences and interests with others. [If you don't believe me, try this experiment. When you meet someone new, see if you can, in *one minute*, find something you have in common other than you are in the same meeting or work for the same company. I have experimented with it many times and so far have never failed to discover something. In fact, I'm amazed at how many people share my dislike for raisins.]

Tell your story first: So often we make the mistake of asking the other person a question, and putting him on the spot. "How did you like the meeting this morning? Did you stay until it ended?" This is more an interrogation than a "trust" builder. No wonder the other person feels exposed and vulnerable. He wonders why you are asking. How should he answer? Is this a test? To avoid this reaction, always start with your own story, making sure it isn't something that puts you in a highly favorable light. Maybe when you attended the meeting in the morning, you slipped out a few minutes early. "I can never stay awake in meetings anyway," you tell him. By disclosing something personal about yourself, you take the initial step toward creating trust.

Ask broad, open-ended questions that give people the latitude and permission to speak honestly and without risk. "What's going on in your job (school, life)?" "How are things with you?" "What's new?" "What's on your mind?" Just the reverse are close-ended questions, which can be answered by a single word, a phrase or sometimes just a nod of the head. They are conversation stoppers. They generally begin with phrases like "do you" or "have you ever" or questions that start with "when" "where" and "who." While there's nothing basically wrong with such questions, they make us seem more like inquisitors than mentors.

With these three steps in mind, I sat down at the small table facing Alicia. She seemed so nervous, absentmindedly tapping on the table, and not speaking a word that I feared she might have misinterpreted the purpose of our meeting. There were no hidden agendas I told her. I was just hoping to get better acquainted. She appeared relieved. I talked about my commute to work that morning, complaining about the Houston traffic, and that bit of small talk seemed to open the floodgates. Alicia told me she took the Park and Ride, a bus service for downtown commuters that originates from key parking lots in the suburbs. She said she got up at 4:30 every morning to make her husband's lunch and take her two boys Roberto, eleven, and Tomasito, nine, to her sister Gina's house. The school bus returned them to her sister's home. Generally, her husband Tomás picked them up in the evening. She said he was a construction superintendent. I told her I had one son, Brad. My husband Paul was also in construction. We were now on common ground.

Before I asked about her work, I wanted to be as open with her as I could about my situation. This is what I like to do when working with someone new. I call it playing fair. Besides, if I were to be of any help, Alicia would have to trust me. While I couldn't hope that would happen the first day, I needed to get things started. So, first I told her about my being concerned about leaving my son Brad, who was "hanging out" at home, waiting for a flash of insight or as Paul put it, a "kick in the pants." She laughed. Then we talked about why I was here. I told her I'd known Elroy Grant for a number of years, and he asked me to come to TYH on a temporary basis. I wanted Alicia to know that I didn't have any idea at this point the way I might make myself most useful, but I was open to suggestions. Then I asked her to tell me about what she did or anything else she wanted to bring up.

Alicia: The Challenge of Overwork

"I work hard," she said. "You saw all the stacks." Then she talked about staying until almost six each day. "There's so much to do," she told me. I found Alicia typical of the hard-working women I have known. No matter how many hours she worked, she told me, she never caught up. In some ways, she reminded me of Sisyphus, a mythical Greek who offended the gods. It was his punishment to continuously push a giant rock uphill. When he got the rock to the top of the hill, it would roll down the embankment, and Sisyphus was condemned to start pushing it uphill once again.

Alicia told me she processed all the orders and dealt with all customer complaints. The rock she was pushing uphill was a continuous flow of paper work, scheduling, and company reports along with the telephone calls from customers that inevitably went to her desk because "she was the only one who had all the pieces of the puzzle."

Alicia was an encyclopedia of information about TYH. She talked at length about their products, the vitamin line, the herbs, the tonics and powders that helped energize, slenderize, revitalize and more. She knew TYH's wholesale customers on a first name basis. She understood the ins and outs of their accounting organizations. Some of the customers were notoriously slow pays, but she would make "courtesy" phone calls to get the paper work and money flowing.

With pride, she described how she kept a record of birthdays, children and other key information on each person she dealt with. She shared this information with the marketers and they used it to keep in touch with customers. "I don't think anyone has ever thanked me for doing it," she added. "Oh, maybe Tom Gaines has. He is such a nice man."

She told me all of this, and when she was done, she looked at her watch and said she needed to get back to work. I thanked her for sharing so much with me, and she went back to her office, to the stacks of paper waiting to be processed and the multiple calls waiting to be returned.

Alicia left me with a lot to think about. I wanted to ask about her relationships with the marketers. I wondered why she hadn't accepted the sales job and what she really wanted. I wanted to know if the massive paperwork had been thrust on her, or if she enjoyed the feeling of being an expert and having others come to her for help. Alicia was a complex person, but I hoped to find a way to relieve her of the rock. It was too soon to open up such potentially sensitive areas, but as we ended our conversation, these questions were on my mind. I wondered how well Charlie knew Alicia and what he could tell me about her at lunch that might give me the start I needed.

Rachel, I'd love to have heard your assessments of us when you first got together with the sugar man. He's a great guy, isn't he! He was with us last night at Oscar's and said to tell you hello.

Hello, Charlie.

He came to the office at 11:30 as promised, asked me if I liked Chinese food and when I said yes, responded, "Good. Let's get out of here." I liked Charlie right from the start, and I could understand why they called him the sugar man. He was fun to be with. He was a short, stocky, round-faced man, and wore wire-rimmed glasses. In spite of his thinning hair, there was something youthful about him. In fact, he seemed like a forty-year-old sprite, not because of his appearance but rather because his eyes twinkled impishly as he spoke.

I was grateful to him because he seemed to sense my need for a friend at TYH, and he had decided to fill that role. "I'm glad they sent you," he told me. Charlie and Ben Turner had become friends, and he frankly confessed that he had called Ben when he learned I was coming. Ben was still recuperating from his heart attack but was getting along well enough to be one of Charlie's poker buddies. "Ben said some good things about you,

Rachel," he said. "Those marketers need someone who has more to offer than marching orders from PWE."

Without revealing the whole story, I told Charlie that Elroy wanted to understand what was happening. TYH was part of his division, and he had made up his mind things had to change for the better, and soon. I frankly confessed I was feeling my way around. Charlie smiled. "I've never had much respect for someone who could parachute in and then offer simplistic solutions to complex problems," he said. "See I like you already, Rachel." When he added, "How can I help?" I could have hugged him.

I told him I met the Powells, and he smiled. "Beth's a sweetheart. Lucien's a good man and he can tell you a lot about TYH."

"I know," I responded. "I'm here for a short time, but I don't want to sit around and watch the place go up in smoke. Before I muck around and make things messier, I'd like to understand what's been happening."

Charlie's Story: Economic Problems of TYH

"In order to figure out what's going on, you need to understand some things about our business. About seven years ago TYH had a rapid expansion program. We went from only one retail store associated with the factory in Sugar Land, to five additional stores: three in Houston, one in Austin, and one in San Antonio. We had plans to enter the Dallas market as well. The wholesale business was focused primarily in three states: Texas, Louisiana, and Oklahoma, but aggressive plans were in the mill to move into Mississippi, Alabama, Florida, and Georgia.

"You'd have to have been here to appreciate the attitude that people had. TYH was a very entrepreneurial place. Griff Lawrence, our President, had a low key management style. There were liberal bonuses and plenty of rewards for high productivity. Gradually, things began to get more competitive in the marketplace, and our Board of Directors heard predictions of doom and gloom from the financial end of the business. Profits were down for the quarter. Building plans for Dallas were underway. There was pressure on Griff to get rid of the retail business and lay off some people. He refused, maintaining things would get better if we didn't overreact and just followed our plan; however, when they didn't improve the next quarter, the Board voted. Griff didn't have the support to maintain his leadership, so they put him on the Board.

"Then, they appointed as president the man who had warned them of disaster, Altis Dunlop, who was our Controller. Altis isn't a bad person. He thought he had the right answer, but unfortunately, he's more of a bookkeeper than a visionary. His first act was to insist that we lower costs to become more competitive. So we franchised the stores in San Antonio and Austin and began laying off people. That's when Griff retired. The speed with which these changes were made had a chilling effect. Costs were dropping and so was morale, but little attention was paid to that.

"At the end of the next quarter, Altis looked at the books and declared we weren't saving enough money. He told each department to reduce its budget by 15%. When managers came back with smaller savings and said they'd reached rock bottom, he created task forces to ferret out waste. We got in the mode of tinkering with things. The more problems we tried to solve, the more we enhanced our administrative bureaucracy, and those costs began to rise. The best raises started going to people who weren't producing but were administering or managing those who were. That led to increased incentives for people to work for advancement. As a result, our best marketers wound up in management."

"Is that what happened to you?" I asked.

"Guilty as charged, ma'am. A couple of years ago we realized that we were moving in the wrong direction. Several consultants later we had adopted some new ideas and wound up flattening, thereby getting rid of the great marketers who had moved into management and reducing incentives related to higher level jobs. At the same time, the competition heated up. The decision was made to franchise our operations in Houston, thus lowering costs and reducing incentives even more. The idea of opening stores in Dallas was dropped entirely. They even considered closing the retail outlet in Sugar Land, but I fought them all the way on that— and won, for now.

"When PWE bought us, people thought things might get better. So far, nothing has changed, so there's a sense of disappointment. I'm probably the only optimist left around, but I think good things are beginning to happen. I've heard rumors that Altis is on his way out. Depending on whom they replace him with, things might improve. So there's my story, Rachel. I'm prejudiced, though, and very close to the scene, so you need to be skeptical. Okay?"

"What happened to the wholesale marketing plans?" I wondered.

"Altis said do it, but of course he offered no extra funds. Can you imagine moving into new markets on last year's budget? Hence, those plans were laid to rest in favor of a more 'financially feasible approach"—his words, not mine. Whatever, the Board bought it, and so we continue our marketing in three states."

I wondered what the impact had been at the Sugar Land plant. Charlie answered simply, "See for yourself." I promised to visit there the following week. Charlie said, "We'll have lunch. There's a great barbecue place out there. You do like barbecue, don't you?" I nodded.

The Marketers: Charlie's Assessment

Then we talked about the Marketers. Charlie knew Tom, Stuart, and Alicia and had recruited Katy. Gayle had recently been moved into Marketing from Distribution, and he could tell me very little about her. "Tom Gaines is a super salesman," he told me, "and finding new business has always been his specialty, but for the last two years he hasn't brought in many customers. You might want to look into that."

"What's your guess?" I asked Charlie. "Is TYH still paying good bonuses? Or could it be something else?"

Charlie said he thought the salary system could be involved, but I would probably learn more by talking to Tom. I agreed. He thought Alicia was a gem. "She doesn't get recognized for what she contributes," he told me.

"Isn't she considered a 'workhorse'?" I asked. "She strikes me as one of those who do the work of three." He nodded. "This may sound cynical," I added, "but *I've rarely seen workhorses get much credit, no matter how deserving they are.* In the beginning, you're in awe. After a while, you start telling them to turn out the lights and lock the doors when they leave."

"You're right," he agreed, "so, why do we let them do it?"

"We shouldn't," I responded, "but I get the impression if I walked into Alicia's office today and tried to take any of her work away, she'd probably feel threatened enough that I'd be lucky to leave with my head."

"She has a college degree," said Charlie. "At one time, I offered her a sales job, but she said 'no sir, no interest, no way.' I got the message. See, I'm smarter than I look."

"Charlie, I refuse to get into how smart you look." We both laughed. "But did Alicia give you any reason for turning you down?"

"She said, 'It's not my thing.'"

"Really? That's puzzling since she knows so much about the products. I'll bet she'd be good. What about Stuart?"

"*Mr.* Kennedy to you. What do you think of him, Rachel?"

"Personally, Charlie, I'm not sure. We've had one meeting, and I got the feeling he wasn't in a welcoming mood. But I'm willing to overlook that and try again."

"Don't expect things to change overnight, Rachel. Stu's got a lot of ability. Right now, it's misdirected. Once, he was Griff

Lawrence's fair-haired boy. He was moving through the organization at warp speed. When Griff left, Stu's upward momentum left with him. I'm not saying he isn't talented. It's just that he skipped a bunch of TYH grades, and he never socialized much with the 'regulars,' so, when Griff left, he was abandoned. Then he developed 'an attitude problem.'"

"That explains a lot," I said. "You know, one thing I've learned over the years. *Over-dependence on one mentor can be deadly*, for just the reasons you described."

"Tell that to Stuart."

"Hmm. So what can you tell me about Katy?"

"Not all that much. I recruited her. She was the darling of her class. I understand she's off to a slow start, but frankly, given all that's going on, I'm not surprised. Someone..." he said looking at me, "needs to take her 'under her wing.'"

"I'm going to meet with her in the next few days. My first read is she's not particularly interested in much I might say, but we'll see. I think I'm going to have to prove I have a decent wingspread before I attract her attention."

Charlie grinned. "You'll think of something. Ben said you were creative and very good with people."

"Don't believe my press notices, Charlie, but I'll give it my best shot."

He drove me back to the office, and we talked of everything but work. How did I like Houston? Was I adjusting to the traffic? What about the family back home? When I told him about Brad, he nodded. "I had one of those boomerang kids myself. Good news, Rachel. He's gone—graduated, and working."

"What's your secret?" I asked.

"He found someone with a 'decent wingspread.' The rest is history."

Judy was waiting for me when I returned. She had set up a meeting with Katy for ten a.m. Thursday and had news. "Gayle's not coming back," she told me. Gayle had called to ask for HR's telephone number and said she was starting her new job Monday. "I took her file off your desk, Rachel. I hope you don't mind, but Personnel needed it to process her resignation. By the way, I don't want to make things rougher on you than they already are, but I've got an interview tomorrow afternoon."

"Thanks for telling me, Judy. By the way, if I can swing it, would you be interested in a permanent job here? If you say no, I'll drop it. If you think you might, then I'm going to call Human Resources this minute and find out if there's any prospects. I'd hate to lose you."

"Thanks for that, Rachel. I might be interested," Judy said, and I gathered that depended on the offer. Fair enough. I wanted her there. I felt supported by Judy, and I appreciated her mature, professional attitude. I realized getting her on the payroll might be a challenge and decided to see how much support there might be from Elroy. Minutes later we were on the phone. "You need all the help you can get over there," he said. "Let me make a couple of calls. If you sense any stalling, call me."

I waited fifteen minutes and called Personnel. TYH had some openings, and later that afternoon they came up with a reasonable offer. Judy was summoned, and after what seemed like hours, she returned with a smile and a nod. I breathed a giant sigh of relief. Hopefully, this would be the start of a good news cycle. Between Judy and Charlie, I was beginning to build a support team, and I knew I needed all the help I could get. I silently thanked Elroy for "greasing the administrative wheels."

My discussion with Charlie had been fruitful, in more than one way. I was thinking about the situation with Brad when I got back to my apartment that evening and called home. Unfortunately, I chose a bad time. Paul was in the midst of a discussion with Brad and told me he would call back in an hour. When he did, I could tell immediately that all was not well. "Do you know how he spent today, Rachel?" Paul asked me.

"He watched television. Can you believe it? He said it was too rainy for a tennis game. That was the last straw! I gave him two weeks. Find a job, register for the next semester, or move. What do you think about that?"

"I think you were generous. Surprised? What did he have to say?"

"Very little. He's borrowed my truck and gone for a ride. He said he'd be home later. I hope I wasn't too hard on him, but this has gone far enough."

I knew things were pretty rough, and I wanted to help. I offered to come home for the weekend, but Paul said things would be fine. "I don't want you in the middle of this, Rachel," he told me. "You have enough people to watch over in Houston. We'll work it out, I promise." I told Paul about my lunch with Charlie and the fact that he had survived a similar experience. His son had connected with someone who had helped him find direction. What Brad needed was someone to talk to. Paul agreed, but neither of us had any idea who that might be. Then Paul suggested I talk to Charlie again to get more particulars about how he had found the right person.

I knew I should wait until tomorrow, but I was desperate, and he was listed in the phone book. His wife answered the phone, and I apologized for calling at night. "Have I interrupted your dinner?" I asked. She assured me they were finished. Laughing, she added, "Charlie will be thrilled you called. He is helping Annie with the dishes, and now he gets a reprieve." Annie was their twelve year old daughter.

When Charlie came to the phone, I told him to pass my apologies on to Annie. "No problem," he laughed. "We were almost finished. What's up?"

I told him, and I could hear the empathy in his voice. "What are you going to do?"

"I'm not sure. I guess I'm wondering how you found the right person to help your son. I'm looking for ideas, Charlie. "

"There isn't much to tell, Rachel," he said. "I told Keith I'd like him to find someone to talk to so he could get another perspective, but it had to come from someone who wasn't a peer. He agreed, but he said it wouldn't be one of my cronies either. For a few minutes we were at an impasse. Then we decided to forget about the specific person and focus on the qualities we were looking for. We wound up with five characteristics. Keith agreed to having the discussion within a week, and I committed to hearing him out without being critical or judgmental and to help in any way I could. Several days later he went back to school to talk with one of the senior dorm counselors with whom he had struck up a friendship. The next semester, he returned to college. The key, Rachel, was in forgetting about who the person was and focusing on the list of traits we agreed on. I think of it as a description of *the mentoring spirit.*"

I wondered if Charlie kept a copy of the list. He said he had some notes on it and would be glad to read them to me, or if I preferred, he would fax them to me tomorrow. I told him I had a paper and pencil in hand.

When he finished reading his notes, I asked one question: did he think the person his son picked, the senior dorm counselor, had all of these qualities? He said he never met him, but his son seemed to think so, and he trusted him. Besides, the results seemed to speak for themselves. I thanked Charlie, apologizing for interrupting his evening.

Fifteen minutes after my call to Charlie, I had e-mailed the notes to Paul and called to find out what he thought. He said he liked what he read and would discuss it with Brad—that is, when they were speaking again. I encouraged Paul to go through the list with Brad and encourage him to modify the language, for if Brad were to have any ownership of the results, he needed to put his own mark on everything. We ended the conversation on a hopeful note, but I must admit the distance made me feel powerless to be as helpful as I wanted to be to either my husband or my son. And although I trusted Paul completely, I wondered whether I should heed his advice to stay in Houston or go home for the weekend. The answer was waiting for me on the internet.

```
From: egrant@pwe.net
To: rachel@pwe.net

    Why don't you spend the weekend with your
    family and meet with me on Monday at ten.
    I'd like to hear more about your adven-
    tures.

    Elroy
```

I wrote a quick reply saying I would be there.

"More about my adventures." That's what Elroy wanted. What I wanted was to convince PWE management that mentoring could rekindle enthusiasm and contribution at TYH. I thought my three months in Houston might be a start. That's why I kept the notes I am going to share with you.

NOTES TO MENTORING FILE

Starting a Mentoring Relationship

It is important to take the necessary time to establish a level of comfort. Building mutual trust is a critical issue in mentoring.

1. Look for common ground: Background, education, the weather, the traffic, family

2. Tell your story first. Disclosing something about yourself that doesn't put you in a highly favorable light is a powerful relationship-building tool.

3. Ask broad, open-ended questions like "How are things going?" that stimulate open discussion rather than more

direct questions like "How do you like working here?" or "What kind of problems are you having?" that make the other person feel vulnerable.

The Mentoring Spirit: Charlie's List

1. **Has credibility** both with the young adult and the parent. That means he/she needs to

   ➤ understand the young person's struggles, having experienced and overcome similar challenges, or

   ➤ be accepted as someone who has helped others or has the capacity to be supportive in some significant way, and

   ➤ be respected for his/her high moral/ethical standards.

2. **Communicates high expectations.** If you want to help someone, encourage her to set high expectations for herself. There is nothing so de-motivating for someone as having those who know her best believe she will not succeed no matter how hard she tries. On the other hand, a large amount of evidence shows the reverse is true, as long as the expectations are realistic.

3. **Is a good listener.** Probably the biggest complaint young people have is that most adults are more than willing to talk to them, but not nearly as open to listening. In particular, that means coming across as understanding but not judgmental.

4. **Has empathy.** Sympathy can make a person feel like a victim because it implies tacitly that he lacks the will or power to act on his own. Empathy can be uplifting. It says we understand another's struggles and at the same time acknowledge the person is capable of solving his own problems.

5. **Offers encouragement without assuming responsibility for the results**—a simple premise, but *fundamental* for someone's personal growth. One who takes on account-ability for another is not acting as a mentor but rather as a doting parent. This deprives the individual of the opportunity to learn from her own mistakes.

With the exclusion of the parent's approval in Item 1, the same qualities apply to mentoring anyone at work.

Chapter 4
Being a Role Model

The real leader has no need to lead—he is content to point the way.

— Henry Miller, The Wisdom of the Heart

I t was Thursday, and I was intent on continuing my "recruiting mission." I knew I was starting at TYH with almost no influence; however, being an optimist, I figured there was no way I could fail since I was already at the bottom.

> *At the beginning, you really didn't have much credibility with us. We considered you a caretaker, someone sent by Perry Winkle Enterprises to hold the line until fresh replacements could be sent in. The problem was, you refused to act like a caretaker.*

No sooner had I entered my office that morning than Judy followed me in carrying `a cup of coffee with cream and sweetener. "You do take both, don't you, Rachel."

I thanked her and told her not to spoil me. "You really shouldn't do this," I said. "I can get it myself."

"I know," said Judy closing the door, "but I thought you might need this fast. Alicia wants to talk with you—right now—and I told her I'd see what was going on. "

I got up. "Judy," I protested, "please don't treat me like royalty. If Alicia wants me, all she has to do is come down or call and I'll.... "

Judy interrupted my oration. "She is on her way. Get ready. She's upset." I opened the door.

"Mrs. Hanson," Alicia began.

"Come in, Alicia, and please call me Rachel. "

She stepped quickly in and closed the door. Then she began to pace. "I don't want to tell on Katy— she's got enough troubles—but I just talked to Frank Manchester from Super Health. He is fit to be tied and threatening to cancel orders."

"Please sit down, Alicia. I want to hear all about it. May I ask who Manchester is?"

"He's in charge of their payables," she replied, pulling a guest chair closer to my desk. "Anyway, they were late paying, and I told Katy about it. I thought she should know." Alicia sat on the edge of the chair, her fingers playing ragtime on my desk. "Mrs. Hanson—Rachel, I always take care of those things, but she was furious and said she would call Frank herself. He said it would take a little time to find our invoices, and Katy, without talking to me first, went over his head, and called John Kramer, his boss. Now Frank's in big trouble, and he said Mr. Kramer was threatening to find a different supplier."

I told Alicia I was planning to meet with Katy today and would find out what was going on. I thanked her for telling me. I could tell by the way she fidgeted there was more she wanted to say, so I asked.

"There is more, "she replied, "but I don't like to be the one...."

"Would it help if I promised not to be angry or upset with Katy?" I asked.

For a moment she hesitated. Then she said, "I've heard other complaints about Katy. People tell me she is quick-tempered and abrasive. I've seen it myself. One time, I got her middle initial wrong on a letter, and she blew up at me. I tried to tell her a couple of times that she should be easier on people, but she seems so—defensive. I know it's wrong to talk about people. She's really a good person, but... I don't know! This is so hard."

She stood up, and I could see her trembling. I walked around the desk and stood beside her. "It's okay, Alicia. I really will see how I can help."

"Please don't tell her I told you this. I don't dislike Katy, but she can be so, so short-tempered."

"You can trust me. In the meantime, what do you think it will take to soothe Mr. Kramer?"

Alicia sighed, "A call from you, I think."

"I'll handle it, just as soon as I talk to Katy, okay?" Alicia left, and I promised to get back to her as soon as I talked with Kramer. Judy was at the computer working on a letter. She looked up. "I'm meeting Katy at ten this morning," I told her. "Has she called in?"

"Yes. While you were talking to Alicia. I didn't think I should disturb you. She said she couldn't make the ten o'clock meeting, but she'd be in sometime this afternoon if that was okay with you. She's calling on The Vitamin Shop. Katy's wearing her pager, so if you want me to I can get in touch with her."

"Can you reach her on her cell phone?" I asked. "I'd like to have lunch with her today at 12:30, if that's convenient. If not, please see if you can set up something this afternoon, the earlier, the better." Judy nodded. A few minutes later, she came to my door. Katy would meet with me at two p.m. Judy also told me John Kramer had called. Things were heating up.

When Judy left, I closed the door and read Katy's file, this time more closely. There was nothing in it to indicate any problems or even any situations similar to the one I had heard about. No one had said she was abrasive or lacked interpersonal skills.

There was also nothing to indicate much in the way of training. Katy had been through the standard three-hour orientation and the mandated time management class. Seven months? Okay, we start from scratch. I asked Judy where Katy's office was. If the door was open, I wanted to peak in, perhaps to get a clue about Katy the person. I promised myself I would go no further. That would be espionage. The door was open; the office was immaculate and devoid of adornment. I'd have to wait until two to learn more.

Around one p.m. I received another e-mail from Elroy. He wondered how the recruiting was going. I replied, "Think in terms of small steps—some forward, some not." His response came minutes later: "Forge ahead—with small steps." I considered what those small steps might be as I thought about my two o'clock meeting with Katy. There were basically four things I wanted to accomplish: (1) to help Katy understand the situation she had created at Super Health (2) to get her to take responsibility for solving it; (3) to help her identify a more appropriate response to pressure situations; and (4) to indicate my intention of responding to the phone call from John Kramer without making her feel I thought she was unable to straighten up her own mess.

I didn't see myself as a supervisor, even a temporary one. There were some duties of supervisors that I knew I would have to perform in the daily functioning of Wholesale Marketing at TYH. It was the larger, more important role of supervisor that I chose to forsake. Supervisors have responsibility for the work output *of the group.* To that end, they give performance appraisals and coach people on performance improvement. I chose not to be involved in that. As I saw it, my role from the beginning was to be a mentor. I wanted to *support their individual growth,* which I believed would impact their satisfaction and ultimately their contribution. The more I discovered about what had been happening at To Your Health, the more convinced I was that mentoring was the only way I might help.

You may be asking, but what of Elroy's charge to recommend the keeping or terminating of the marketers? My response is simple. Right or wrong, I had already made up my mind I would recommend that all stay, and unless I found a major insoluble problem, I had no intention of changing my mind. That fit with my personal philosophy that when organizations foster personal growth, provide opportunity, and expect accountability, people usually rise to the occasion. In the short time I was to be at TYH, my focus would be on growth. My responsibility was to make that answer the right one. Based on what I had seen already, I had no illusions it would be easy.

Katy: The Challenge of Interpersonal Behavior

Promptly at two, Katy appeared. I jumped up from my chair and invited her in. This afternoon she looked striking, dressed in a red suit which showed off her dark-skin and wearing her hair in a single long braid. At five feet ten inches, she towered over me. When I asked her to sit down, she perched on the edge of one of my blue guest chairs, and I had the feeling she was getting ready to fly off. I remember thinking this discussion would not be easy. To my invitation of coffee, she responded brusquely, "No thanks, I don't drink caffeine." She refused soft drinks and water as well. "What's up?" she asked me. I couldn't quite understand how it happened, but in short moments since she arrived, she had quickly assumed command of this meeting.

"About Super Health..." I began.

Katy interrupted. "Under control," she told me confidently. "They'll be writing us a check today." She stood up. "Anything else? I've got to write up an order." She spoke in a voice both resonant and commanding.

"Yes," I said. "About Frank Manchester..."

"What an incompetent!" Katy said dismissively, shaking her head to accent her disapproval.

"Super Health is a long-standing customer. Now they're upset, and...."

She stretched out her arm, fingers up, palm facing me in the kind of gesture traffic policemen make when they want you to put on the brakes. "I'll handle it."

That's a gesture that irritates me, but I took a deep breath and continued. "That's fine. It's yours to handle. Now, please sit. I need some information from you before I return John Kramer's call."

She sat down, slowly and reluctantly. "He called *you*? What for?"

"I haven't talked to him yet. I wanted to meet with you first. Help me out and tell me what you think he might be wanting, Katy," I said.

She seemed to sink into the chair. "Okay, Rachel," she said with a sigh, "I agree that I might have come on a little strongly when I called him, but Super Health is my problem, and I want to straighten it out myself."

I silently checked off items one and two. "Listen, Katy," I said taking another deep breath, "do you think I've never spoken when I should have been listening? That I haven't used a tone I regretted? I understand how you might have been exasperated by problems with the account, but you can see what happens when you go to battle. It doesn't matter who's right or who's wrong. Now everyone's defenses are up. I've been there and I've got the scars to show for it. Take it from me, as a very wise man once told me when I stepped over the line, negotiating will get far better results than confronting." *I have always found it much more convincing to admit having made my own mistakes when advising another how to correct hers.*

"I'll apologize if that's what it takes to make everything all right," said Katy with a sniff, "but my heart won't be in it—I can tell you that."

"I understand," I responded, "but a graceful apology is what's called for, don't you think? A friend of mine calls that 'falling on your sword.' It's a great image, but apologies aren't nearly as fatal."

"Sounds like suicide to me."

I laughed. "He's done it a number of times, and I can report he's still alive."

For the first time, I saw the hint of a smile. "I'll call Frank right now," she said.

"Do you think it might be better to wait until I talk with John Kramer?" I asked. She sighed, then nodded. "Why don't you call him in the morning? If it's okay with you, we could meet around eight, and I'll tell you what Kramer said."

"Let's make it 8:30," said Katy, asserting command once more as she sprang up and headed for the door.

"That's fine. In the meantime, let's both keep in mind the outcome we're looking for."

"Outcome?" she asked, turning toward me.

"Restoring a warm relationship with Super Health and expediting their invoice payments."

"Sure," she said, as the door shut behind her. So I called John Kramer. At first, he sounded aloof, but after I "fell on my sword," he began to soften up. Then I discovered he knew Elroy Grant. That cinched things. They had met on an airplane when both were attending a conference in Rio. By the time they parted three days later, they were friends. Kramer shared a few Elroy stories, and I added a couple of my own.

Then Kramer turned to the subject of Katy. "Don't know about her," he said. "She's a pistol." I pointed out that Katy was very knowledgeable but relatively new to the business world. Kramer told me he hoped I would "straighten her out," and I promised him we would get things resolved. Our conversation was friendly enough, thanks to Elroy. At the end of it, I felt Kramer was in a watchful and waiting mode, but I was pleased he made no further threats to cancel orders. I dropped by Alicia's office and told her that I had spoken with both Katy and John Kramer.

"What about Frank?" she asked.

"Katy is going to call him in the morning," I told her.

"Will she apologize? Will it be all right?"

"Yes to both," I responded. "And thanks again for coming by." I looked at my watch. It was 4:50. I walked to her door. "It's late Alicia, and you've put in a full day. Let's close up shop and go home."

"But I have some things to do."

"I'll bet they can wait 'til tomorrow, "I said smiling. "I'll be in my office. Come by and we'll walk out together." About fifteen minutes later, Alicia and I left the building. Maybe, it wasn't a major triumph, but it definitely was a beginning.

On the drive home I reflected about the day. Even though both meetings, the one with Katy and the follow-up with Alicia, had gone reasonably well, I was under no illusions that major changes would ensue. Basically, both women had recognized that I had some authority, albeit temporary, and I had not overstepped the invisible boundary they had set for me—at least not yet.

I stopped by the grocery, picked up some fragrant teas, and brought a bouquet of white and pink carnations for Lucien and Beth. They had finished dinner when I knocked on the door and presented the flowers. Beth insisted that I come in, have some tea, and taste the results of a new peanut butter cookie recipe. I was delighted; the cookies were still warm from the oven. As we munched on them, I filled the Powells in on the situation with Brad.

"Are you going home for the weekend?" asked Lucien. I said I was, even though I had some misgivings because Paul had told me not to come. Beth felt that Paul might not have wanted to trouble me, but she was sure he would be glad to see me. At times like these, we could be great support for each other.

Then we talked about TYH and what was going on there. When I told them about my lunch with Charlie, Lucien nodded. "I've always thought a lot of Charlie," he told me, "and so does everyone at TYH. He may be unassuming, but don't underestimate him, Rachel. He has a lot of influence. If you need something, he's your man."

"Like what?" I wondered.

"Information, service, getting things done, whatever—a word from Charlie generally stops the foot dragging."

"Sounds like superman," I said. "Can he leap tall buildings?"

"Maybe not tall ones," laughed Lucien, "but he has leapt over the TYH Building a time or two."

"Perhaps I should ask him why all the walls are undecorated and painted white," I said. "I think it's depressing."

Lucien's Story Continued: The History of the White Walls at TYH

"Oh, I can tell you that. I still have my spies over there," Lucien said chuckling. "Several years ago, when your company was coming to look the place over prior to buying us, Altis Dunlop, our President, walked around the building and saw a couple of offices that didn't look business-like enough. There were pictures of children and a few by children, dried flowers in frames, etc. on the walls. In one office, someone had shelves that were painted blue or yellow and had decorated with large paper flowers. Anyway, Altis decided that the building needed to have a 'clean' business-like look. So word came from the president's office we would be painting and re-carpeting. The painting was done the following weekend. Mysteriously, the shelves were painted white, those wall hangings that hadn't been removed by the tenants disappeared, and there was a notice in the middle of everyone's desk to the effect that everything on the walls had been warehoused. Personal belongings, including the paper flowers, could be reclaimed there and taken home. Any pictures people wanted to put back on TYH walls would have to be approved by Human Resources. I heard folks were pretty angry, and most of them rebelled at asking permission to put something on their walls. But tell me, Rachel, why are you so concerned about what is or isn't on the walls?"

"Because I believe that the walls are symbolic of the unresolved conflict that has hurt productivity at TYH. Management has a right to set some standards about the appearance of the work place, but it sounds as if this was handled by fiat. And then, instead of suggesting standards, they made matters worse by requiring people to go through a bureaucracy to do something as simple as hang something on their walls. In my experience, people usually react to what they interpret as unfair punishment by withdrawing the most intrinsic asset a company has, personal productivity. It's like what happens in a family. When we impose our will on others, sometimes we fail to see that silence is more destructive than openly-aired conflict. It's amazing to me how little attention is paid to the small things that matter so much to people."

I told Lucien that I suspected TYH management had chosen to ignore the silent rebellion, and two years later people no longer cared, but I sensed a lingering hostility in the air. I wasn't sure that doing something about it would have a major impact, but I was convinced it would be a good start. The two things I was sure of were (1) that I couldn't face those bare walls much longer, and (2) I wasn't planning on reinforcing the current situation by seeking approval to hang some pictures. Actually, I wasn't sure the rule was still in effect, and I decided right then I wasn't going to go through a bureaucracy to find out.

* * *

It was Friday and I was looking forward to going home for the weekend. I felt a bit guilty, I admit, since I had so much to do here, particularly since I still hadn't finished arranging my small apartment and giving it at least the semblance of home.

I waved to Judy in passing and headed straight for the coffee room. Stu and Katy were in the midst of a conversation, and for some reason I thought I might be the subject, particularly when the unfinished sentence, "You don't have to..." seemed to die on his lips as I entered the room. Quickly moving to the door, Katy mumbled something about seeing me at 8:30 and left. Stuart followed me back to the office and stood in the doorway. "Got a minute?" he asked.

I nodded, and he entered about two steps and then leaned on the wall, one hand holding a cup of coffee, the other, in his pocket. A rather sophisticated, debonair look, I decided. Refusing to sit, he said he'd like to meet with me later and asked if he should make an appointment through Judy. "No," I responded, "let's set a time right now." We agreed on 2:30, and I suggested the small conference room across the hall.

At 8:25 I headed for Katy's office. For the first few minutes, we spoke of everything but the reason I was there. I told her briefly that I had returned Kramer's call and that he had indeed been annoyed. I felt the relationship was in limbo, depending on how things went with Manchester. Katy told me she had been giving the whole situation some thought and wondered if an apology were really necessary. "You know, Rachel, we were in the right," she said adamantly. "If Super Health had kept their promise to pay when they should have, none of this would have happened."

I agreed, adding, "Even so, now it has happened, and we could lose their business. What do you propose to do?"

"I don't know, but I think it's like a thunderstorm. If we give it some time, it'll blow over. "

"Katy, is this your best idea, or is this about your reluctance to talk to Manchester?"

"Oh, I'll be glad to talk with him," she said, repeating the 'stand back' gesture that had irritated me the previous day, "but I'm not so sure *he* doesn't owe *me* an apology. Imagine saying he couldn't find the invoices. If I've ever heard a lame excuse...."

"You have a good point, Katy. Mind if I suggest another way of looking at things?"

"No," she shrugged. "Go ahead."

"Okay, let me try. We have a long standing relationship with Super Health, and they've been slow-paying for the last month or so. Right so far?" She nodded. "Think of it as you would a family relationship. There's been a misunderstanding with some angry words spoken. The question isn't who's right or wrong; it's what do you do now? Let it fester? My experience is that even in families, that can create situations in which people who care about one another may not speak for years. On the other hand, if the person who spoke those words, no matter how justly, apologizes for the things he or she said, that facilitates a return to a normal relationship where problems can be worked out. Do you agree with that?"

"Yes, I do, Rachel, but this is nothing more than politics. Why should we let them get the upper hand?"

"I'm not sure I'd call this politics, "I replied, "but, in a sense, you could argue that all relationships are political. I know you're not married, but you have an older brother who is, right?"

"Yes. He's eight years older than me, and he has a wife and two adorable children."

"Okay, Katy. Now when Thanksgiving and Christmas come around, doesn't he have to negotiate with parents and in-laws relating to where they spend the day? That's politics, albeit family style. Anyway, that's my way of looking at things. So, if it were up to me, I'd call Manchester. Yesterday, rightly, you told me this was your problem. It is, and I'll leave the decision on how to handle it up to you," I said rising.

"Okay, so I'll call him up and say I'm sorry that he took offense over my call."

"Ah, the legal apology."

"Legal?"

"Yes, Katy. In my opinion there are essentially six ways to apologize; five meaningless games and one gracious way."

Avoiding an Apology: The Five Meaningless Games

"Five meaningless games?"

"Sure, first there is the *legal* game—it's when you transfer the blame to the other party. You're pleading not guilty. So you say 'I'm sorry that you took what I said the wrong way.' Then there's the *journalistic* approach. That's the so-called apology that attributes everything to an unnamed source. 'I was told you had handled this. That's why I reacted so strongly.' Who's lying? Who knows? Should you take forty percent of the blame? Thirty percent? Why not take a poll? Third is the *scientific* apology. In this one, you hold the whole event under a microscope, agonizing over each detail. Did A lead to B? Was there a scientific cause behind it? You say 'I did X because you did Y. Perhaps if you had done Z...' Get my drift?"

Katy laughed. "I think I've done all of those at some time."

I laughed too. "So have I. That's why I can name them all. The problem is, when I've used them, I've never gotten the result I wanted."

"I can see why. So what's next?"

"Next is the *theatrical apology*. 'Oh, I can't believe I could have done something so awful. You wouldn't believe what was going on here. I mean, it's a zoo! Can you ever forgive me?' Finally, there's the *political* apology. In this one you talk as if something may have happened, but no one was there. It goes, 'We regret a mistake was made by someone. Of course, since we had no control of the situation, we can't assume responsibility for the event.'"

"Okay, Rachel. Let's say, just for hypothetical reasons, you were going to make a gracious apology. What would you say?"

Role Modeling

"Whenever I have something like this to do, the first thing I think about is the *outcome*. Yesterday we talked about what a good outcome would be—an improvement in the working relationship. I mean, here's an opportunity, so why not take advantage of it? So, the first thing I'd say, *if it were me*, is 'Frank, the reason I called is that yesterday I messed up (or lost it, or goofed) and I'm sorry.' I like *'goofed,'* personally, but pick your own word. Then I'd give him a chance to respond. Let's say he told me the whole thing made him angry. Then I would say, 'I don't blame you for being angry. I should not have called John Kramer, and I certainly hope he wasn't mad at you.' If he told me Kramer was angry, I would say, 'Rachel has called him and let him know we were out of line. If there's anything more we can do please tell me.'

"At this point, I would expect him to either be generous and nice or still a bit huffy. Either way, I would ask him if there were some way we could help him research the invoices. If not, would he prefer we send duplicates. I would also tell him, if there's a problem at any time in the future, please let me know, and I promise to handle it better."

"What if he's still huffy?"

"My position is always this: *I make one good sincere apology.* I do not keep apologizing for any offense, no matter how awful. If someone needs that, my feeling is he should 'lighten up.' The key is, no matter what, be gracious, but don't revisit the crime scene. Just act as if everything is okay, and move on. If you follow this strategy, all will go well, believe me. But don't forget, Katy, *an apology is only useful if it's followed up by action.* After all, in most cases, it's possible to make amends. Some people go on committing all kinds of small atrocities and behave as if an apology makes everything all right. I know that's not you, Katy."

"No, it's not. I'm off to make a gracious apology, Rachel, and to make amends. I'll let you know how it goes."

"I have no doubt it'll be fine."

Stuart: The Challenge of Cynicism

By 2:30 I was sitting in the conference room waiting for Stuart. When he didn't arrive by 2:40, I stood up to leave, and opening the door, almost collided with him. Unfortunately, some of the contents of my diet coke wound up on the front of his starched blue shirt.

"Oops. Sorry," I said, flinching inwardly at the sight of brown speckles on his shirt. "I had given up on you."

He paid little attention to me as he took the tissues I offered and wiped at the stains.

Then he turned toward me. "Did you know you got it on your dress?"

I looked down at my dress and laughed. "Well, I feel better then. We match." He laughed too. What he wanted to talk about he told me was the possibility of his moving into Perry Winkle Enterprises. Opportunities at To Your Health had dried up with the downsizing and flattening of the organization. He was too young to sit things out, he said. I told him PWE expected continued expansion in the next few years. He pressed me. I said that Elroy Grant would probably pay us a visit in a few weeks and I'd be sure to introduce him.

He wanted to know how well I knew Elroy. I responded that I had known him for a long time and had worked for him several times. Then I asked him to tell me more about himself. He said he had always had aspirations to move up in the organization. He thought things were going well but then Griff left. Now that PWE had shown some interest in being more than a distant owner, he saw some possibilities for the future.

Stu let me know he was no stranger to corporate politics. He wanted me to talk to Elroy about him. I told him it was probably premature, but I'd see what I could do at some time in the future. When I pointed out we'd have a stronger case with Elroy if the group could improve marketing results at TYH, he looked at me as if I had just arrived on a space ship. "Here?" he asked, incredulously.

I felt as if we were not having a conversation but rather taking turns talking. I asked him what he could tell me about the marketing problems at TYH. He shrugged and said he had lost interest. "Everything has fallen apart," he said, adding, "you probably won't be hanging on to Katy much longer. She's much too good for this place. Gayle stayed in this department just two months and quit. Marketing at TYH is the kiss of death."

He had thrown down the gauntlet. I struggled to moderate my reaction, but inwardly I thought If Elroy heard him today, he'd be history. "Why is that?" I asked.

"Because everything has shut down. Maybe no one cares anymore."

"No one?"

"Well, maybe not everyone," he responded.

I didn't understand. It didn't appear that everything had shut down. The company was still in business, I told him, and the PWE plans I had seen indicated it was likely to remain so. I pressed him. "What about your sales?" I asked. "Can you tell me how they are going?"

"Okay," he said. Then looking at his watch, he said, "I've got to go. Big weekend plans. Maybe we can finish this next week. I'm hoping you can give me more insight into the opportunities at PWE."

I agreed, then added, "Think about the situation at TYH. Maybe you can give me some more insight into what we need to do to revive things here." He nodded and left me with a gnawing sense that the team, at least his part of it, had already left the field. Stu was a double concern to me. Judging from what I had seen and experienced, he had influence on Katy. I hoped his attitude wasn't poisoning hers.

Around 3:45 I heard some voices outside my office. It was Tom Gaines talking with Judy. I got up and went to the door. "She's here to stay," he said, smiling and motioning toward Judy. "Good work, Rachel."

"It's Judy who does the good work," I said and he grinned. After today's events I thought it would be nice to talk with someone who wasn't ready to do battle, so I invited him in. He was on his way to a meeting he told me, and then in a stage whisper added it involved happy hour at a bar close by. We talked about the weekend, and he told me he and his wife were taking some customers to a basketball game. I told him I had a plane to catch.

As I got ready to leave, I thought of Alicia. Could she still be at her desk? I made up my mind she was leaving, like it or not. She was still there. "Let's walk out together," I said. She started to protest, then began cleaning off her desk. "I'm coming, "she said and looking straight up at me, she smiled.

My flight was late departing, and so I passed the time at the airport putting some notes about the day into my laptop.

NOTES TO MENTORING FILE

Sometimes mentors need to be teachers, especially when the person being mentored is relatively new to the business world. It is important to explain the reasons for recommending specific actions as well as giving examples when asked. The art is to teach gently without philosophizing. It always helps if you can empathize by pointing out your past shortcomings in the same area. What have you learned? Don't be hesitant to respond to the mentee's concerns or answer her questions—about politics, or anything else.

Example: Making an Apology

1. When making an apology, first consider the outcome.

2. Say you're sorry, admitting *you* messed up. Don't try to make yourself look good to avoid blame.

3. Acknowledge that the *other person* has a right to be angry (or confused or disappointed, etc.).

4. Make amends.

CHAPTER 5

Mentoring through Difficult Situations

I don't know the key to success, but the key to failure is trying to please everybody.

— Bill Cosby

I remember feeling vaguely dissatisfied with the weekend, not because of Paul but rather because little seemed to be happening with Brad. Our son was in and out, doing his normal weekend things. Once I saw him head for the car with a pair of in-line skates tied over his arm. This did not look like progress to me. Paul was getting impatient, but he said we should give Brad a little more time. The discussion between them had gone well, Paul told me, it was just that nothing had happened since. Brad had said he would think about it. Given the fact it was only two days since then, we both decided to give him the benefit of the doubt. He would come through we assured each other.

Monday morning arrived all too quickly. I smile thinking about it as I pick up the letter and reread the passage:

> *When you didn't come back that second Monday, I thought we had run you off. Judy was out that morning, but when she came back she assured us that you were visiting the main office. Aha, I thought, plotting!*

I must admit I was plotting. I told Elroy of my preliminary assessments, starting with the meeting with Altis. He listened intently. "He's on his way out, Rachel. I spoke to him yesterday. He'll get a good retirement package, but I left him with no illusions about the future. No matter what he does, it will have to be somewhere else." Elroy told me they had not yet decided on a replacement. There were several candidates at TYH, but Elroy thought bringing someone in from PWE might be a breath of fresh air. I told him that PWE was seen as an absentee landlord and little else. He nodded in agreement. "That's over," he told me. Then looking straight at me, he asked, "What else?"

I told him I was troubled by the building and its antiseptic, temporary look. Somehow, it seemed to be symbolic of the lack of energy and boredom I had seen at TYH Headquarters.

He nodded, "You've mentioned this before. It's time to change things. Check out your budget."

"What if there isn't money available?" I asked.

He rolled his eyes. Then he said, "Did you lose your company credit card?"

We both laughed. I brought him greetings from his friend John Kramer of Super Health, telling him there had been a slight misunderstanding, but leaving out the specifics of the situation with Katy. Then things got serious. I told him TYH's decision to pull back on both wholesale and retail marketing coupled with

Altis' management style had morale at rock bottom. He said he wasn't surprised, adding that PWE had spent too much time studying the situation and not enough doing something about it. He said he was thinking of paying a visit, but he wasn't sure when. "I've still got some unfinished business with Altis," he said, "and besides, I'd like to take a look for myself."

Then he asked me what I thought of "my crew."

I told him people were demoralized from all the changes that had occurred. Gayle had left, and I thought we needed to replace her. Elroy agreed, pointing out that was one of the few supervisory duties that couldn't wait for my successor.

"We've got to get your team up and running," he said. "So what about the others?"

I told him Alicia was a "workhorse" and probably could make a more significant contribution. "She really cares," I said, "but she'll burn out if she continues working the way she is now." I thought Katy had potential, but she needed some interpersonal coaching and training.

He grinned. "It's good that you're there. She couldn't get it from a better source."

"The problem," I grimaced, "isn't the coaching or training. It's convincing her that she needs it."

"Well, according to my friend and interpersonal guru Rachel, that's always the monumental task, isn't it?"

"Guru? Me?" We both laughed.

Tom Gaines was well-liked, I continued, and I hoped we could find a way to encourage him again. Then I spoke of Stu. "I'm not sure what to think, Elroy. He was considered a hotshot once, but now he's disgruntled, and it's rubbing off on Katy."

"Think we should let him go?" Elroy wondered.

"I'm not sure yet," I said (and I was surprised at my response, because I had been thinking that was just what I wanted). "I'd like to see if we could bring him back because I think some of what's going on with him is TYH's fault. On the other hand, I could use some advice from a pro."

"You're the pro, Rachel."

"You're not getting off so easy," I countered.

"What were you thinking of doing?"

"I'm not sure. I want him to understand how his attitude is affecting his credibility and future. Just as important, I want him to stop pushing Katy toward the edge. The problem is, my talking to him might increase his defensiveness and cause worse problems."

Preparing for a Difficult Conversation

"I think that depends on what you say to him. At this point, he isn't a very likeable fellow, and that could be standing in the way of a good dialogue. Maybe the way to approach him is through the door he's already opened—that is, what he is looking for."

"He knows I can't give him what he wants, except through you."

"But you're my surrogate, Rachel. So why not tell him why you're there? You've been sent by me to assess the situation and make recommendations about the people. Tell him you're stuck when it comes to him. Then, hold up that mirror. Here's what you see, and here's the impact. He's got options, and you can talk about that. You know 'the drill.' Heck, you've taught it to me. Just let him know the outcome is in his hands."

"You're a genius. That'll work."

"You're going to have to be direct. He's not a kid, and he's looking to move up. Tell him the truth. That's treating him with respect, whether he likes it or not. Just be sure he understands what you're talking about. From what you're telling me, his days with TYH are numbered if he doesn't shape up."

"Agreed. But I'm not promising when we'll talk. I need to find the right moment."

"As long as he doesn't destroy your Stanford graduate, that's okay. Just don't drag it out. I'm guessing that's more advice than you were looking for. How about a quick lunch in the cafeteria?"

I was having lunch with Paul I told him, but I took a rain check. Before I left, I asked when he planned to visit TYH. "I'll await a formal invitation," he said.

"From?"

"You," he told me. "Keep the e-mail coming." I said I would.

Paul and I had lunch on the way to the airport. We reassured each other that things would go well with Brad. Paul promised to call the minute he and Brad talked, and I left to go back to Houston.

* * *

Tuesday morning was sunny and crisp, one of those perfect Houston days you wish you could keep in the freezer and thaw when you needed it. I took Memorial Drive enjoying the collection of brightly clad joggers, walkers and runners, accompanied by an assortment of Labs, Dobermans, and Rotts, all getting their morning exercise. Ahead and slightly to my right was the skyline, an elegant asymmetric display of rectangles and pyramids in mixtures of glass, granite and marble. In the car immediately in front of me was a woman eating a doughnut. Immediately to my right was a man driving a Lexus and reading the newspaper. I decided it was his car, but I was pleased when my lane speeded up and I passed him. No time to waste. Houston was getting ready for work.

I thought about my plans for the week. I wanted to touch base with Judy and see how things were going. I needed to call HR and start a search for someone to replace Gayle. I wanted to find out from Katy how the discussion had gone with Frank Manchester. I wanted to set up some more time with Alicia to continue our discussion. I planned to call Charlie and find out when I could come out to Sugar Land. I wanted to meet with Tom Gaines and get his thoughts about marketing. You can see how my mind was working. I wanted everything but a meeting with Stuart. I was busy, and besides, I needed more time to think, I told myself.

Judy wasn't at her desk, so I went to my office and checked my e-mail. A brief note from Katy assured me she had made contact with Frank Manchester. She said all was well, and she would fill me in later. I went by the coffee room, and Judy was there making fresh coffee. "I'll do that," I told her.

"I'm just about finished," she replied. "You can get it another time."

Fair enough. Judy had called Personnel Monday to see if they had any candidates for the opening. She had that level of initiative you pray for and seldom find. There were three folders sitting on my desk waiting for me, but first I decided to drop by and say good morning to Alicia. She was just hanging up the phone as I walked in. "Rachel, you won't believe it," she told me, "my husband thinks you're a miracle worker for getting me home before 6:30 two days in a row."

I smiled. "Well, please thank Tomás and tell him that I'll believe we worked miracles when you start leaving before five and getting *me* to walk out with *you*. Deal?"

"Deal," she said, smiling back.

"When can we get back together?" I asked. "I think we need to continue our discussion about you and what you're looking for."

"How about this afternoon," she responded. We agreed on two p.m., and she said she preferred to meet in the small conference room. I promised to reserve it.

I passed by Katy's office, but she wasn't there so I returned to mine. As I looked through the three folders, I noted all were TYHers who wanted to move into Marketing. They were from Human Resources, Accounting, and Distribution, Gayle's former home. The person from Distribution had a Marketing degree, which seemed to make him the best choice. Before I made a decision, I decided to talk with Tom Gaines and find out what he considered to be the qualities I should look for and ask Charlie Rothstein if he knew any of the candidates. I felt this research was necessary not only because I wanted to pick the best candidate but also because we were experiencing enough bumps in the road without additional problems.

Charlie was in and extended an invitation to Sugar Land for the following day. I would drive out there in the morning and tour the plant. Charlie promised to fax me a map but only if I agreed to stay for lunch and eat barbecue. "Okay," I said, "I'll wear something dark." He laughed and said he'd see me at nine.

I called Katy and left a message on her voice mail. Then I asked Judy for Tom Gaines' cell phone number. He was on his way to take a client to lunch, he told me, and wouldn't be back this afternoon. We made plans to meet Thursday morning. My calendar for the week was filling up, and I was aware I had left Stu off of it—deliberately. No, I said to myself. This is not going to happen. I will see him, and I will talk to him by the end of the week. Not good enough, I thought. I'll call him now and see when we can get together. He's going to wonder why. What shall I tell him? It's about picking up our conversation from last week, I decided. The initiative was mine, at least for the moment. If it became his, we'd pick up the game where we left it. New rules! Let's quit fooling around and get a conversation going. I picked up the phone, and he answered. When I hung up moments later, Stuart Kennedy and I had a meeting scheduled for Wednesday afternoon at 3:30.

Later that morning I dropped by Human Resources. The manager was Lily Sheldon, a genteel and proper lady who shook my hand limply and invited me to sit down. Her lips seemed permanently pursed, and she reminded me of my junior high school principal, Mrs. Steely (whom we used to call the iron maiden). She made the usual inquiries about my situation: apartment, finding my way around Houston and all the rest. I made the necessary small talk—weather, traffic, and housing.

I was really there for one thing—to satisfy my curiosity about how her office was decorated. The answer was tastefully. The furniture was French Provincial, and she had elegantly framed period art on the walls. So did her assistant, Mary Alice. Looking up and down the hall, the Human Resources group had obviously policed themselves into very attractive surroundings. I had seen no evidence of this anywhere else in the building. Part One of my grand plan was in place.

I was heading for Katy's office when Alicia stopped me. She was distraught. She and Katy had had words about last week. "What specifically?" I asked. As I suspected, it concerned the Super Health situation. Katy had walked into Alicia's office and told her she didn't appreciate Alicia's "ratting" on her about Manchester. I could see she was near tears. She said Katy owed her an apology. "Rachel, I told you she was quick-tempered," she said. "This just proves my point."

I was inclined to agree, but I didn't want to make matters worse. We went back to my office to talk. "I have a lot of respect for your interpersonal skills, Alicia," I told her. "If you could picture how you would want this situation to come out, what would that be?" I had already gathered what Alicia would prefer, which was for me to step in and squash Katy like a bug. She was tapping again, so I knew she was nervous. Nonetheless, I believed any interference from me would just put off the inevitable showdown. Alicia said she'd like to have a better working relationship with Katy. She described it as one in which she and Katy could discuss problems without Katy "jumping all over her."

We talked for a few minutes about Katy's being new to the business world, and I reiterated that she needed Alicia's help. Alicia, after all, was good at relating to customers, and that was a skill Katy needed to develop. I encouraged her to give Katy some feedback about how she came across, particularly in stressful situations. The key was to confront the problem, not the person. "After all," I added, "you two are on the same team." From the way she was chewing on her bottom lip, I got the impression Alicia was a bit annoyed as well as understandably apprehensive. She had come in wanting me to solve the problem. Now she knew that wasn't going to happen, she frankly confessed that she wasn't sure how to approach Katy. She asked me if I had any ideas to make things go better. This is what I suggested:

When Giving Feedback Is Going to Be Hard

"*First*: Ask Katy's permission to give her feedback. Talking to her without her agreement is a waste of time. So say something like, 'May I talk to you for just a minute about this morning?'"

"Suppose she says *no* or that she's too busy?"

"Tell her you think it's important to clear the air and ask her when the two of you can do this. Be persistent.

"*Second*: Show her that you are looking at the situation from both sides. Say, 'I can understand why you might have felt unhappy (upset or frustrated) about what happened with Frank Manchester.' It's very important to focus on the *immediate situation* here.

"*Third*, tell her what you'd like to talk about and describe the benefit. 'I'd like to talk about what happened between us because I think we could have a much better working relationship.'

"*Fourth*: Let her know the impact of her behavior. Now here's a key point, Alicia. Don't tell Katy she was abrasive or defensive. Those characterizations always make matters worse. Instead, describe the defensive behavior. For example, 'When you interrupt or make a stopping gesture with your hand, it makes me feel as if you don't want to hear what I'm trying to tell you. Then I feel like saying, 'What's the use?'"

"But what do I do if she jumps down my throat again?"

"It helps if you are prepared for it. After all, it shouldn't be a surprise. Isn't that the very thing you're there to talk about? To be fair, once you outline the situation, you need to give her a chance to respond," I said, *"but keep the discussion focussed on the problem you two are having with communication.* Point to how she's responding right now. See what I mean? Above all, do not get drawn into a discussion of the Manchester situation. Tell her that until you two find a way to communicate, there's no way you can discuss it. Your being firm about this will help Katy understand there are penalties for overreacting."

"Penalties?"

"I'm not talking about being punishing. There's a difference. Penalties are not 'pay back' like punishment is. Penalties are simply predictable consequences. If you were playing football and stepped out of bounds, the result is the forward motion of the ball stops right there. That's a rule of play. *Feedback should never be punishing. It's just information, helpful information, delivered from one imperfect person to another about something that can be improved or, at the very least, changed.* Now, if you have problems resolving this issue between you, I'd like to step in and facilitate the discussion. I think it's that important."

"Why not just do it that way in the first place?"

"Because you and Katy are the two who need to work this out. Are you willing to try?"

She sighed. "Okay, but I don't like confrontations."

"It doesn't need to be a confrontation. It's an opportunity to practice your skills and to improve a relationship at the same time. My experience has been that being open and honest is a good way to resolve differences and a key business skill." I added, "As for the Manchester situation, there was no way to keep it quiet, Alicia. Don't forget, Kramer called me. Your warning was helpful because I wasn't surprised by his call. However, as promised, I never told Katy that you said anything to me."

She nodded.

"Are we still on for this afternoon?" I asked.

She sighed. "I hope I can get something done today," then added, "I want to talk some more about my work so let's get together at two."

"I'm going to see Katy to find out what happened with Manchester," I told her. "I want you to know, Alicia, that I'm not planning to bring up what's going on between the two of you. That's up to you. Pretend she's one of your customers and do your usual stellar job."

A slight grimace. Then, "I'll do my best."

My discussion with Katy was brief. Yes, she had spoken to Manchester, and things were fine. In fact, he had found the invoices, and a check would be on its way this afternoon. He too was sorry for the misunderstanding and invited Katy to come out and visit. Not a word was spoken about the discussion with Alicia—by Katy or by me.

When I returned to my office, Judy told me that Alicia had stopped by. She was feeling swamped. Judy had rescheduled our appointment for Friday morning at ten. She hoped that was all right with me. I nodded. Then I sat down and wrote up some ideas for our meeting. Alicia was very orderly, and I thought this might give her time to collect her thoughts. In some ways, I was adding to her "rock" but it seemed to me a rational process for chipping away at it. First, I asked her to describe her role, adding, "Please don't tell me what you do, but focus on why TYH has you doing those things." Next, what, in her opinion, added the most value and what was not worth her time? Third, what part of her job did she most enjoy and why? Finally, what were her aspirations for the future, short and longer-term?

I ran off a copy and took it by Alicia's office. She was reading a paper from one of the many on her desk. She looked up and started to apologize for changing our meeting. I smiled. "It may turn out to be for the best. I've got a few questions for Friday. Please, please don't feel you have to write any answers to them. It's a working document to help us both focus on what's important." I turned toward the door, then back to Alicia. "If you want to put down some questions and give them to me, I'll work off your list." She nodded. Just then the telephone rang, and she turned toward it. I went back to my office.

That night Paul called. When I learned there had been a setback with Brad, my heart sank. Paul had come home about two to pick up some things he had left at home and found Brad and a couple of his buddies in-line skating in the street. "Rachel, I made up my mind this had to stop," he said, with a tone of outrage. "I didn't lose it," he said, "at least visibly, but I asked Brad if he'd mind coming in and talking for a few minutes. He told his fellow teenagers he'd be right back. When he came in, I told him I wanted him to work with me for the next few weeks or months while he was 'deciding' what to do with his life. He said I shouldn't worry about that—he'd found a job."

"A job? What about school? What about talking with someone about his future?"

"He doesn't need to go to school for this job, Babe, and he's obviously not worried about his future. He's going to be a manager-trainee at a fast-food place, one of those drive-ins that specializes in hot dogs and hamburgers. He says for a year he'll work all the jobs and fill in while he learns the business."

"The business? I can't picture him cleaning the rest rooms."

"Neither can I, but it's better than playing kid's games all day."

"Well that's not exactly my dream for him, but what do we do now? He's not moving out, is he?"

"He hasn't said. I told him fine, if that's what he wants to do with his life, go for it. He told me he might want to own a chain of them someday. The boy has absolutely no idea of what things cost. Anyway, I treated the whole thing as serious and said I wanted to see him committed to something worthwhile and important. If this was it, fine. Was he prepared to make a six months commitment?"

"Six months? You didn't!"

"I did."

"I don't want him working in some hamburger palace for six months. What about school? What about doing something meaningful with his life? What about Charlie's idea?"

"Hold it, Rachel. Let's let this thing play out. Right now he's having trouble making a commitment for the weekend, so don't fret about the six months. Brad will be all right. He's our son, isn't he?"

For the moment, I wasn't sure.

When I hung up, I brewed a cup of hot tea. Paul was probably right, and I was acting like an over-zealous mother, or was I? To take my mind off my son and his career aspirations, I decided to make some notes based on my meetings with Elroy and Alicia. I wondered if Alicia would confront Katy. I felt it would be good for both of them. Katy could benefit from some feedback and Alicia would grow in her skills to handle conflict.

NOTES TO MENTORING FILE

Working through Problems

When the Issue Is the Person Being Mentored

Mentors need to have *respect* for the people they mentor. This is a relationship between two adults, which requires honesty on both sides. Remember, *your role is to help the other person find a solution to his problems.* The first and most difficult step is generally convincing the mentee that a problem exists, so don't assume there is agreement on this.

➤ Hold up a "mirror" and let the person see what his behavior looks like.

➤ Give your *opinion* on how others might be reacting.

➤ Share your own similar experiences, if any.

> Help the person review his options, including the pros and cons.

> Offer advice *only* if the person asks for it.

When the Person You Are Mentoring Has Problems with a Co-worker

As a mentor, you should resist two pitfalls when the person you are mentoring has a problem with a co-worker. *First, resist the urge to take sides*, either by engaging in gossip about the other person or chastising the one you are mentoring. Instead, acknowledge the difficulty and be empathetic. *Second, avoid offering unsolicited advice.* Act rather as a consultant. Ask open-ended questions that focus attention on the desired outcome. "So how would you like things to come out?" In that way, you are helping the mentee learn two things: how to handle such disputes and how to find solutions by focusing on the problem, not the person. Sometimes your advice may be requested.

Example: Advising the Mentee on how To Give a Co-worker Feedback

1. Ask for permission to give feedback. If the other person isn't willing, stop immediately. Unwelcome discussions generally increase tensions rather than help to alleviate them.

2. If necessary, agree on an alternate time. Be friendly, but persistent.

3. When the time comes, focus EXCLUSIVELY on the *immediate situation*. If the problem is you have a hard time talking about your differences, then talk about the communication problem, not the differences.

4. Tell her what you'd like to talk about, describing the benefit.

5. Disarm the other person by showing her you see the situation from her perspective. "I can understand why you're angry about this."

6. Let her know the impact of her current behavior or actions, suggesting alternatives.

7. Be willing to admit your own mistakes or contribution to the problem.

CHAPTER 6

Collaboration and Conflicts

> *A stander-by may sometimes, perhaps, see more of the game than he that plays it.*
>
> — Jonathan Swift

The next morning I set out for Sugar Land. To Your Health's production facility was on a four acre site. The first thing I noticed driving in was the colorful array of purple and blue pansies and white periwinkles leading up to the front of the red brick Administration Building. For some reason, the thought of my barren office with its sterile white walls immediately flashed through my mind.

To the left of the Administration Building, standing in the middle of a grassy area with stone benches, were two flag poles, one flying the American flag, the other, the Lone Star flag of Texas. Beneath the Texas flag was a green and white TYH flag. To the left of the flag poles was a large replica of a thermometer bearing the news that TYH was moving toward seventy percent of its United Way goal.

I entered the building through the glass doors and found myself in a small reception area and lobby. Charlie had left word to expect me and when the receptionist called his office, he was there in under five minutes, carrying a green windbreaker. "This is the latest in office wear," he grinned. On the front was the TYH logo. On the back was the motto: "High Quality Products For a High Quality Life." "If you make the whole tour, and you tell me you've never had better barbecue, Rachel, you'll go home with one just like it. In fact, I'll throw in a couple of 'gimme' caps for Paul and Brad."

"So you've guessed, I can be bribed." We both laughed.

We started off the tour in the main building, which housed administration, along with offices for personnel, safety, training, and maintenance. There was a lunch room with kitchen facilities, a large meeting room, and a small conference room. I was struck by the startling difference between the atmosphere here and that of the downtown offices. A bulletin board in the coffee room was brimming over with cartoons, family pictures and personal advertisements from people who wanted to give away kittens, sell cars and boats, or find furniture and housing. As we walked down the hall, people emerged from their offices to be introduced or to tell Charlie something. Even more important, I heard laughter. "Okay, Charlie, I give up. What have you done to make such a difference?" I asked.

"Not me, it's them," he said smiling. "And distance, most of all distance."

The main building had wings on either side. On the left side was a To Your Health retail store. We walked in, and I was pleasantly surprised by how busy it was. Some customers were checking out, their baskets loaded with vitamins, minerals and other health care products. I saw several people at the shelves, reading labels and others looking for specific items. There were three TYH employees there: one at the check out stand and two assisting customers to locate particular products. "Is it always this busy?" I wondered.

"Almost," said Charlie. "This store does very well."

"Why did management want to close it?"

"They were closing everything else. There gets to be a rhythm to it."

"You fought to keep it open, didn't you?"

"I had to. One of the greatest satisfactions people from the plant and the lab get is coming in here and seeing their customers–close up. See that woman over there, the one with the baby and toddler? Well, that's why we're so dedicated to quality. Sometimes I go over to the plant and encourage the supervisors to send people over here just to remind them. On slow days in the plant, the supervisors often get employees to work a day shift here. It's good for them." I could see why Charlie was so effective at what he did. He understood how to make the important connections for people.

Our next stop was the lab which occupied the right wing of the building. It was bustling, and big signs announced only forty-four days left before the introduction of a new product line. There seemed to be almost an air of celebration there, and I was eager to tell Mr. Kennedy that "the news of TYH's death" hadn't reached this group of dedicated people.

Finally, Charlie took me through the plant, and I was impressed by the efficient and sparkling clean facilities as well as the quiet hum of activity. No wonder Mr. Rothstein had invited me to see for myself. I asked Charlie how often company management came from headquarters to visit the plant. "A little too often," he grinned.

Using a Network

Later, when Charlie and I were having lunch at Red Barron's Barbecue, he asked me what was on my mind. I told him I missed the brightness of the offices at PWE. I loved flowers and pictures and found they lifted my spirits. I thought TYH head-quarters offices had a very cold and sterile look. The marketing area certainly didn't inspire me, and I wanted to do something about it. I had heard he understood how the "system" works at TYH. I was looking for budgeted money. Here was my di-lemma—I wanted to do some decorating, but I didn't want Human Resources to make decisions about what we could and couldn't do.

"I don't think you'll have a problem with Lily," Charlie said, speaking of the Human Resources Manager.

"Maybe not," I responded, "but somehow, Charlie, I think it's important that we stand up. I get the feeling everyone down-town is in a prone position. There's a defeated attitude there, and I thought a minor rebellion of sorts might shake things up a bit. I don't want to create a revolution though. That's why I'm talking to you before forging ahead."

He nodded his understanding and suggested we go back to his office where he kept "all the confidential info." It took less than five minutes for Charlie to find the answer.

"If you were permanent, you'd have $3,500 to spend on your office."

"I am permanent," I said grinning, "just not perma-nently here."

"Next question."

"What about the marketers? Is there money for decorating their offices?"

"You'd have to get that out of the Department's budget."

"I guess that means a visit with Accounting, right?" he nodded. "Okay, Charlie, here's where you come in. If you were looking for a 'friendly person,' someone in Accounting who gives advice and isn't intimidated by the 'picture police,' who would you call?"

"That's easy. Ron Corbin. He's Assistant Controller. When I need to understand what leeway I have or chat with a good financial counselor, he's the one I call. In fact, Ron keeps me working. I have to earn enough to pay the ten dollars I usually lose to him at our Thursday night poker games. Would you like me to call and tell him he needs to meet a friend of mine?"

I happily accepted Charlie's offer knowing that his good opinion would help me start the discussion with Corbin off in the right direction. Then we talked about Gayle's replacement. I told him I had three candidates, but I was leaning toward one in particular. Before I made a decision, I wondered if he knew any of them. He looked through the three folders offered by HR as possible replacements for Gayle. "The rational choice might be Robert," he said, pointing to the folder of my top candidate from Distribution. "However, if you're not looking for a Stuart Kennedy sound-alike, you might be more interested in my first choice, Justin Graves from Human Resources."

Charlie told me Graves was a twenty-six year old who had started at one of the TYH retail stores in Houston. When the store became franchised, he had transferred to the Personnel Department in Sugar Land. That's where Charlie had met him. While he didn't know Justin very well, the encounters they had had were pleasant and friendly. "He's an intelligent young man with a great personality. He'll do fine in Marketing, Rachel," he told me. Two years ago, Lily Sheldon had transferred Justin into Headquarters HR. "The word is, he's got a bright future," Charlie told me. "I'm looking at him for a job in the plant after he's had some marketing exposure, so you'd be doing me a favor." The third candidate, Mary Simms, was a possible candidate too, but I noticed Charlie sounded a bit lukewarm about her. Friendly, personable and shy is the way he described her. The Marketers would have her for lunch.

It was a little after two when I got back to TYH Headquarters, carrying one green jacket and two caps. There were several call slips on my desk. One was from Lily Sheldon, the HR Manager, probably concerning the candidate folders on my desk. Another was from Ron Corbin, the Assistant Controller, and more important, a friend of Charlie's. Those were two pleasant distractions from the 3:30 appointment I was not looking forward to. I promised myself I would return both calls later, but my most important task was to get ready for Stuart.

Conflicting Agendas

Whenever I have something really sensitive to do, I like to think about what I want to accomplish. I didn't think either Stuart or I were ready for a "cut to the chase" meeting. That would probably happen soon, but we both had ground work to do. The purpose of this meeting was to (1) get better acquainted, (2) explain my role, including Elroy's charge to me, and (3) get Stu's assessment of what was happening or not happening in Marketing. With such a reasonable agenda, I felt we could begin to make some progress.

Promptly at 3:30 we met in the small conference room. We greeted each other and shook hands solemnly like two diplomats preparing for a strategic negotiation. The first five minutes were spent in small talk. How was his weekend? Did I have a good trip? What did he do last weekend? How were things in Oakville? Then, almost as if the bell had rung and we had dispensed with the formalities, Stuart jumped in.

He'd been thinking about my questions regarding why Marketing was in the doldrums and had come up with a plan. It involved his travelling to Oklahoma and Louisiana as well as San Antonio and Austin to visit "old" customers. Then he would go to Mississippi, Alabama and Georgia to develop new business. While he was in Georgia, he thought he might take a side trip to Oakville and perhaps, with my help, meet Elroy Grant and see PWE, which was now, after all, his home company.

As he spoke, I saw my carefully planned agenda disintegrating before my eyes. "Okay," I thought," let's head off in this direction for awhile." I asked him to go back to the first part of the plan. What did he expect to accomplish? He replied, he wanted to get better acquainted with customers. How long did he expect such a trip to take? He thought about two weeks, give or take. Then we turned to the second part. I wondered if he had thought about which businesses to solicit. From his response, I gathered he hadn't gotten that far yet. But still, it wasn't a bad idea. In fact, it was the first plan I had heard anyone come up with yet. It's just that I wasn't sure whose problem he was trying to solve: TYH's or his. In any case, I thought his idea deserved a fair hearing—so I asked him to put a brief proposal in writing. Now I've known many a manager who did that as a means of stalling. That wasn't what I was doing. I'm a person who likes to think things through. That means if someone, anyone, demands an immediate answer from me, it's almost always *no*. On the other hand, this might turn out to be a good plan, and a carefully thought out proposal would help it along.

Stuart didn't see it that way. In fact, I could tell he was plainly irritated. He said, "We are in sales aren't we?"

"Of course, we are," I responded. I was not opposed, I wanted him to know. In fact, I believed meeting with customers would pay off. It was just that I felt these trips would require some coordination. I also felt others on the team would want to be included. I asked him to get everyone together to talk it over. Visibly annoyed and shaking his head, he started to leave.

"Wait a minute Stuart," I said, still seated. "I hope you don't think I'm trying to frustrate you. I want to help in any way I can."

He turned back toward me. "Then don't be a roadblock," he replied. "That's the trouble with this place. Too many people saying *no*." He left.

I sat there for a full five minutes sorting through my thoughts. Had I been too rigid, too demanding? I had a problem with his attitude, and he had a problem with mine. Should we have had it out, right then and there? I had no reason to doubt myself, but there was something about Stuart that left me feeling frustrated and guilty. It's as if he had somehow shifted the burden of his problems to me, and something in me had been all too willing to accept them.

I left my concerns in the conference room and returned to my office to call Lily Sheldon. The decision on filling Gayle's job was not yet made, I told her. First, I was going to consult with Tom Gaines. When she learned I was leaning toward Justin Graves, she expressed surprise, reminding me that the Distribution candidate, Robert Darman, had more qualifications in Marketing. I asked her if there might be a problem if I chose Graves, and she quickly assured me there would not be. She had included him because she knew him to be interested in Marketing. He'd been a very high performer in Human Resources, she told me, and she really hated to let him go. "I understand," I responded. "He sounds like someone we'd be interested in." I promised to call the next day.

I was starting to dial Charlie's friend, Ron Corbin when I heard a booming voice just outside my door. "Look what I've got for you, Rachel," said Tom Gaines holding up two steaming cups of coffee. I instantly abandoned my telephone call in favor of a friendly face.

"I thought you weren't coming back today," I said.

"Changed my mind. And here I am," he said offering one of the cups to me. "It's fresh," he added, "and you need it."

"And why is that?"

"Because you look up tight," he replied.

"What makes you say that?"

"Your jaw is set, your shoulders are almost up to your ears, and besides, I saw Stu leave the conference room about half an hour ago. He didn't seem like a happy camper to me, so I went out looking for the wounded."

"I'm fine," I said, but he wagged his index finger back and forth and smiled.

"Don't tell that to Dr. Tom. He knows all, sees all, and says nothing—usually, but you're a pretty nice person, Rachel, and I'm sure you feel as if you've walked into a nest of vipers. Kind of like an Indiana Jones story. Lots of adventure and you don't know what you're going to run into around the next corner."

I laughed. It was easy to see why people were taken with Tom. "Stuart wants to make a road trip, but before he goes, I just want to be sure what the lines are between yours, his, and Katy's territories. I'm all for visiting, but I'm hoping the results will be there. So this isn't a stop sign, just a caution light. Anyway, Stuart is going to get everyone together to work something out."

"Thanks for that, Rachel," said Tom. "I'm not keen on having Stu, or anyone else for that matter, visit my customers."

"Speaking of customers," I said, "Charlie tells me you are world class at bringing in new business."

"Did he now?" asked Tom. "And did he also tell you it's been a while?"

"Has it?" I asked as if I were unaware. "What's going on?"

"Nothing," said Tom, "and that's the problem." He got up as if to leave.

"I'm sorry," I said. "Sometimes I can be a bit thick but I just don't get it."

"We still on for tomorrow?"

"Yes, at nine."

"We'll talk about it then. Right now, you need to relax and enjoy your coffee. Trust me. Dr. Tom always knows best."

"Bye Dr. Tom," I said to his retreating back.

He turned, just for a moment. "See you," he said smiling.

To: egrant@pwe.net
From: Rachel@pwe.net

Mirror images: Houston and Sugar Land. One
is formal, stiff and over-managed; the
other, a study in leadership. I am continuously amazed at the impact a warm, open
style has on people.

Rachel

To: Rachel@pwe.net
From: egrant@pwe.net

Why do you think I sent you there?

Elroy

CHAPTER 7

Generating Enthusiasm and Energy

> *The three great requirements for a happy life are: something to do, something to love, and something to hope for.*
>
> — Joseph Addison

Oakville, Georgia. Last night as I slept I returned to TYH and those absurd white walls. In my dream I gave every one of the Marketing Group a handful of Magic Markers in assorted bright colors and asked them to put graffiti all over the walls. Justin drew a big red clock and Katy was working on a rainbow. We were all having a grand time drawing pictures, writing, laughing and joking when Lily Sheldon, dressed in a policeman's uniform showed up. She was swinging one of those billy clubs like a keystone cop and shouting, "Put those markers down, put them down." But we ignored her and kept drawing. Then she took out a whistle and began blowing in shrill ear-piercing sounds."

I was startled by four paws landing in the middle of my abdomen. Chula, our tiny blue Chihuahua had jumped on the bed, and Billy, our handsome black and white one was scratching and whining to get up. The door to the bedroom was slightly ajar. Paul hurried in. "Did my whistle wake you? I wanted to let you sleep, but they made a beeline for the bedroom. You must have stayed up late last night."

"I did," I confessed. "I was dreaming about TYH and particularly about the walls. I think it was the letter that brought it all back."

Rachel, when you get an idea, it's fun to stand back and watch. You're an artist at making things happen. In fact, I think your specialty must be jostling people out of their complacency.

It's funny how vividly you can recall certain events in your life. I remember the day after my trip to visit Charlie in Sugar Land. I was energized by what was going on at the plant—and particularly intrigued by how much difference that setting was from the one I had encountered at TYH headquarters.

Thursday morning started with my regular visit to the coffee room. Judy had already made the coffee, and when I start to point out to her that I was going to do that, she smiled. "I like to make it. Then I can be sure there's the right amount of coffee and water. I'm very particular." Properly chastened, I decided she wanted me to drop the subject, and so, after filling my cup, I returned to my office and called Ron Corbin.

104

Funding the "Wall Rebellion"

We exchanged small talk about TYH in general and Charlie in particular. Finally, Ron brought up the subject. "I understand you're looking for money."

I appreciated his directness and told him so. "This place looks like a morgue, and you can't separate the sleeping from the dead in this environment."

He laughed and said he agreed, noting he was generally oblivious to his surroundings. He told me I had $3,500 to spend adding, "What about the person who follows you? He may not like your choice of art."

"I think that person, whoever it is, would rather find some energy in the people here than worry about wall decorations. If I can't square it with him or her, I'll see what else can be done."

"Next question."

"But can I spend that money anywhere on walls? I mean, does it actually have to be in a specific office area?"

"Strange question. I guess it's up to you to define what your office area is."

"My problem is $3,500 isn't quite enough. We've got seven offices, so I'd need roughly $7,000, that is, counting the $3500, and that's minimal. So where else in the budget can I get more money for decorating?"

"Have you talked with Lily? "

"Is she the only one who can release funds, or is she the resident decorator?"

"Neither one. I just don't know whether the orders have changed around here about what goes on the wall."

"I understand. Do me a favor, Ron," I said, "I don't want to know what the orders were, so please feel free not to tell me."

"You got it." He added, "I've looked at your budget, and I think you could squeeze another $2,500 out of it. By the way, have you checked out the warehouse? There's some stuff there, and it mightn't hurt to be sure there's nothing there you could use."

"How do I know it doesn't belong to someone?" I asked.

"I wouldn't worry. If people haven't claimed it by now, they've lost title." When I asked him how to get there, he suggested I get Judy to call Betty Lee, Altis' administrative assistant. "She has the keys."

"One more question about money. If I need more, should I plan a bake sale or is there a bucket buried somewhere?"

Ron laughed. "How are your chocolate chip cookies?"

"Thanks Ron," I told him, "I'll pull out my recipe book. Seriously, I want you to understand that I'm not planning on starting a revolution around here. It's just that sometimes some minor civil disobedience can help wake people up. This sound minor enough to you?"

He laughed. "It does, but don't take that as my giving you permission. I've heard Altis will be leaving one of these days, but until he does, I'm covering myself. By the way, call me when you get the pictures up. I might bring my troops around to take a look. Who knows. Your minor civil disobedience might result in the beautification of our area as well."

After we hung up, I talked to Judy about the project. She offered to visit the warehouse and report on the quality of what was available. If it was worth a field trip after that, she'd let me know. At nine, I heard noise outside my door. It was Tom. He and Roger, one of the mail clerks, were roaring with laughter. Minutes later, he was at the door. "You want to meet in here or in the conference room?" he asked.

"Your choice."

"I'm not afraid of the lion's den," said Tom. "Let's talk here." I came around my desk and we sat facing each other in the blue guest chairs.

Tom shared a couple of jokes that had passed the "Roger test." "If he likes them, I tell them to everyone. If he doesn't, they go in the trash. Roger has a sensitive ear."

"They passed the Rachel test, as well," I told him. Then it was down to business.

Did I really want to understand what was going on at TYH, he wondered.

I said I did.

He asked me how much I knew about the last five years at TYH, and I told him Charlie and Lucien had both filled me in on the general outline. Where my interest now lay was in what had happened in Marketing.

Tom's Story: The Salary System's Negative Impact on Marketers

So he told me. What I heard was that each change sent shock waves through the company. The Marketers were entrepreneurs, and the old TYH as run by Griff celebrated their success. The more you produced, the higher the rewards were. Then Altis decided to remove commissions and put everyone on a salary. Coming from a financial background, he reasoned the certainty of a moderate rate of pay would be far more attractive than taking a risk for higher rewards. The new system was incredible. Part of the marketer's salary included a one to ten percent bonus provided he reached an ever-moving sales target; so basically, he was paid ninety percent of his projected salary and had to scramble for the rest. This new salary system had removed the impetus for most of the group to perform at their highest level. (This was my introduction to TYH's salary system. I was to understand even more about its impact as time went on.) Then I asked, "What about you?"

Tom, the Challenge of Motivation at the End of a Career

"I guess when I turned fifty-two, Rachel, I looked around, noticed some of friends were having heart attacks, and decided it wasn't that many years before I'd be leaving. So I said, what the heck."

"I can understand that, Tom, but in some ways you're shortchanging yourself. I don't have any idea how long you plan to work, and it's none of my business. It's just that even three years is a long time to coast, especially for someone with your talent."

There was a silence. "So what can I do for you?"

I smiled. "Glad you asked. I need some advice. We're going to fill Gayle's position. Did you know that?" He nodded. "I have great respect for your knowledge and experience, Tom. You're a born salesman, and you know what it takes to be successful. There are several candidates for the job. One comes with a Marketing degree and is in Distribution. The other doesn't have those credentials. He has a background in HR and has worked in our retail business and at Sugar Land."

"And?"

"Well, I have heard the Distribution person might be a bit cynical. I haven't met him, but this is what I've heard, and I trust my source. The HR candidate has a reputation for being a team player, but I'd like to hear how much weight you'd give to the credentials and how much to the personality."

"Ideally you'd like to find someone with both. I'd say it's a toss-up, boss, but if it were me, here's how I would analyze it. You can teach anyone to sell, but you can't change personalities overnight."

"That's basically what I'm hearing from Charlie too. Do you know Justin Graves?"

"Sure. He's on the company softball team with me. I didn't know Lily would let him go. Human Resources has designs on him."

"From what I understand, so does Charlie."

"If it were me, I'd bring him on. He'd be great."

"Well, there's more. Don't tell me right now, if you think the answer might be *no*. Tom, would you be willing to take Justin around with you, teach him to sell?"

"You mean for a week or so?"

"No, I mean until he's good—really good—as long as that takes. It could be one month; it might be three months, whatever you think!"

Tom frankly admitted he was intrigued with the idea of teaming up, just as long as he could decide how intense the association would be and how long it would last. I asked and received permission to add an amendment. He and Justin would make that decision, together. So, it was agreed. I had my reasons for asking Tom. He was good—the best, and Justin could learn a lot from him. At the same time, I believed that Tom could benefit from a fresh perspective.

And then there was the matter of a legacy. One of the most important things that happens at the tail end of most careers is the person begins to consider what part of himself he wants to leave behind. This is not an unusual thing to do. A number of good friends near retirement have reported this phenomenon: One day you're doing your job. The next, you're picturing an imaginary cornerstone of the building with your name on it. I say imaginary because the contributions that become a legacy usually are not etched in granite. Rather they appear in people, in policies, in the subtle changes that prove you were there and made a difference, no matter how invisible.

I snapped out of this reverie when Tom returned to the subject of customer visits. "Rachel, Stu has a good idea. I do think it's time to make the rounds. If Justin comes in soon, he'd get a good start by visiting customers."

"Especially with you," I added.

He stood up. "Why don't I get together with Stu and Katy off line. We'll kick things around without raising anyone's hackles. Got any problem with that?" I smiled inwardly at the enthusiasm I was finally hearing in his voice.

"None whatsoever. Sounds like a good plan to me."

"I'll let you know how it goes." He put out his hand and shook mine. "You're not bad," he said, "for a Perry Winkler."

"Neither are you," I responded. The meeting was over.

```
To: egrant@pwe.net
From: Rachel@pwe.net
```

I'm beginning to see some sparks of energy
around here. Good sign. Stuart's idea about
visiting everyone's customers has recharged
the competitive spirit. Tom is taking the
challenge, and as for me I'm just watching
the fun. Alicia is gearing up to contest
Katy's manner a bit, and you'll never guess
what I'm doing. I'm on the sidelines with
encouragement and Band-Aids.

Rachel

```
To: Rachel@pwe.net
From: egrant@pwe.net
```

You are exactly where you need to be, doing
just what I knew you would do. Keep doing
nothing in the way only you can. Add some
iodine to your expense account.

Elroy

Immediately after my meeting with Tom, I called Lily. I wasn't sure how transfers were handled at TYH, but at Perry Winkle, now would be the proper time for me to meet with Justin Graves. After such a meeting, the wheels would turn, either quickly or slowly depending on how much work was left on his desk and who might do it. TYH was a much smaller company than its parent, so I didn't know how they would backfill Justin's desk, but my hope was that if all went well, we could have him here in the group and under Tom's tutelage within two weeks.

Apparently Lily had gotten over the first shock of separation anxiety because she offered to send Justin down to my office for a preliminary talk. When could he actually move? Lily surprised me by saying the middle of next week. I learned later that quick moves were typical at TYH, confirming my belief that there are some real advantages to life in small companies.

First Impressions of Justin

I had no sooner hung up and started for the door when I saw him. Tall and slim with sandy brown hair, Justin reminded me of the young son I had left at home. He was bending over Judy's desk, and she was rifling through some snapshots. He straightened up as I approached and put out his hand. It wasn't long after we were seated in the two overstuffed chairs that I too was handed the pictures. A pretty blonde woman lay in the hospital bed holding a baby boy in her arms. Justin, who looked barely older than Brad, was a new and very proud father. Was I old enough to be a grandmother? No, not quite—but for a moment I was not in the office interviewing a young man who might join our group, but miles away in my own home and with my own family.

Our conversation was brief. I learned that Justin had moved to Headquarters about two years ago and that he was eager to do something that would help him grow. He wanted to make a bigger contribution, he told me. Above all, I was struck with his natural interpersonal gifts. I liked him immediately for his warm, friendly, inquisitive, and courteous style. Instead of the typical questions I had answered ad infinitum, he wondered about what kind of work I had done in the past. When he learned I was an organizational effectiveness consultant with PWE, he was eager to get my perceptions of TYH. We both had an HR background and were on common ground easily. Justin freely confessed he would have much to learn in this new job, but he told me he was an eager student and if he came to the group, he would really appreciate my perspective on how he could improve. "I don't mind constructive criticism," he told me, "and I wouldn't want you to be too easy on me."

For my part, I was convinced that he would be a great addition to the group because of his attitude. We talked about his working with Tom, and Justin beamed. "He's a pro!" he told me. The meeting over, I called Lily. Protocol required that she be the one to inform him he was moving to our group. We agreed to have him report here Wednesday, and I made a note to ask Judy if she would check out his office and make sure he had what he needed by then.

Minutes later, as I walked out the door to talk with her, I caught a glimpse of Stu engrossed in conversation with a thin bearded man in the hall outside Judy's reception area. Neither acknowledged my wave. Just then, Katy walked up to them and I heard her call him Robert. This greeting, unlike mine, was acknowledged by the pair in the hall and the conversation continued in low tones as Katy joined them. I surmised that was probably Robert Darman, the candidate from Distribution offered up by Lily.

I turned back to Judy who was visibly pleased with my choice of Justin. "Isn't he something?" she asked. "Everyone likes him." She quickly agreed to check out Gayle's old office. Then she held up a card key. "This is to the warehouse," she told me. "I'm going over there this afternoon to see what pictures are available. Want to go with me?"

Before I could respond, I heard Katy's voice behind me. "I do," she announced. When Judy suggested all three of us go, I thanked her but demurred, citing my schedule as the reason. It wasn't that I didn't have the time. I saw changing the appearance of the department as basically a TYH undertaking, and while I was committed to making it happen, it was far more important that the people who would be staying here make the decisions. I was delighted that Katy was interested in the project. Judy asked if there was anything in particular they should look for. My vote, one of seven, was that whatever was selected, or bought, I hoped would be bright and cheerful. When I went back to my office, I heard Katy and Judy laughing together as they planned their afternoon.

Right after lunch, I looked in on Alicia. I knew we had a meeting the next day, but I was wondering if she and Katy had talked. She shook her head. "I've been too busy," she told me. I could not criticize her in my heart, for I knew that Stuart and I were yet to have a meaningful conversation.

Later that day Judy and Katy returned from the warehouse carrying three small pictures of the Sugar Land plant and a Houston skyline photograph. "Slim pickings," said Judy.

Katy frowned. "You wouldn't believe what they had in there. Old, old, old. I don't blame Mr. Dunlop for having them removed."

"Altis," I said. "He may be the president, but I've noticed it's the practice here to speak of everyone by first names."

"Okay, Altis. Whatever. Anyway, I don't want any of those," she said, wrinkling her nose and pointing at the pictures Judy put down on her credenza.

"These will be extras," said Judy. "They'll fill in if needed. If not, back they go. So what's next, Rachel?"

"Let's think about how to pursue this," I said. "Any ideas?"

"Why not bring someone in from one of the local shops, tell all of us what our budget is and let each of us decide what we want?" suggested Katy.

"Sounds good to me," I replied.

By the look on her face, I could tell Judy had other ideas. Katy and I waited patiently. "I think we should adopt some sort of a group theme for this. We agree on some guidelines and then let everyone choose what he wants from within them."

I was afraid that sounded a bit too much like a return engagement of the "picture police." Both Katy and I preferred total freedom of choice, but in the spirit of teamwork, we agreed to put it to a vote. Judy would send out an e-mail and tally the votes. Then we'd move on to the next step of bringing someone in to help.

I went back to my office to do some paperwork. Time ran away from me and when I looked at my watch, it was 5:30. I would have to hurry to be home on time. I wanted to freshen up a bit since I was having dinner with Lucien and Beth. But first, I stopped by Alicia's office to see if she was still working. There was a note to me on her door. It read, "Bye, Rachel. I left at 4:30. I passed by your office but you were on the phone. See you tomorrow. Alicia." Progress!

The Minor "Wall Rebellion" Continues

That night at dinner, I told the Powells about my decorating plan, confiding that I wasn't sure $6,000 could cover seven offices, but I was committed to making it work. Lucien was delighted. "Let me get this straight, Ms. Philanthropist. You mean you're breaking with tradition and not taking the $3,500 for your office?"

"That's right," I said, "and before you scold me about using the money of the person who might be coming in, let me tell you, I've cleared this with Elroy. We'll furnish the money for any additional decorating if necessary."

"I'm not about to scold you. I was thinking of giving you a medal," Lucien said laughing. "You're about to set the administrators with all their rules on their ears. Good work, Rachel. And don't let anyone put a guilt trip on you about the money," he added more soberly. "This is nothing new. Use the money. Enjoy it. If TYH has to cough up a little money next time, believe me, it won't break 'em. Most times, when someone comes in, they spend about $5,000 on their own offices, no matter what the budget is, and no one says a word. I'm surprised Charlie didn't tell you that."

Beth said, "I hope you don't mind if I offer a suggestion, but I have a friend, Marie Janek, who has a Frame Shop. She does lovely work. I mean, she's a real genius and she won't take advantage of you. Feel free not to use her, but if you

114

like, I'll have her contact you tomorrow. You'll love her—and she's reasonable."

Lucien said, "Take my word for it. If my wife says she's reasonable, she's downright thrifty. Beth is the thriftiest person I know."

"Now Lucky, don't give Rachel the idea I'm cheap. I'm just a good shopper, that's all."

"Well, cut me a piece of your delicious orange cake, and I'll shut up," he said.

"How about you, Rachel."

"I'll shut up too," I promised. Everyone laughed.

When I went back to my apartment, I thought about how lucky I was to have met Lucien and Beth. They were such a delightful couple. Something ached inside of me. I called Paul. When I heard his voice, the aching stopped. Brad was out with some friends, squeezing a lifetime of fun in before his first work day putting patties on the grill. I shook my head. I wasn't coming home this weekend, I told him. I was a bit tired and thought I'd catch up on my rest. "Well," said Paul, "you're about to have some company. I'm lonesome and I'm flying down for the weekend. And don't plan to meet me. I'll catch a cab and see you Saturday morning around ten." My spirits lifted.

CHAPTER 8

Asking the Right Questions

A prudent question is one-half of wisdom.

— Francis Bacon

The next morning was a late September Friday in Houston, Texas, and the sky had arranged a rock concert complete with the rhythm of staccato rain, lighting effects, and intermittent drum beats of thunder. I was on my way to work and more in need of quiet chamber music. Traffic crawled along, but my head was racing. Quiet music on the radio, thoughts of the weekend with Paul and unfinished business with Brad, Stuart, Katy, and Alicia competed for my attention. My agenda was not too detailed that day, but I was on edge.

116

Instead of my usual cup of coffee, I made some hot tea and focused attention on my meeting with Alicia. This time I wanted to talk about the rock. She had made important contributions to Marketing, but I was convinced she had more to offer and more to receive. It's funny about people like Alicia. We think of them in the most utilitarian way. They add to our comfort, they take care of the many details that are keys to our success, and yet we realize how vital they are to us only when they go on vacation or get sick. So, we accept their hard work, we smile, we say the right things, but secretly we are content to let the Alicias of this world go on pushing that rock because we know that if they don't do it, we may have to pick up a piece of it. And sometimes, without intending it, we thoughtlessly add to the rock because we know they won't resist.

At ten I was in the conference room. No Alicia. I went to her office, and she was just hanging up the phone. She looked up, grabbed a pad and walked toward the door. "Conference room?" she asked. I nodded and followed her brisk steps down the hall.

I knew immediately that she felt stressed, especially when the tapping started. "Alicia, can you give me an hour?"

"I don't know. I hope so."

"I'll take a completely focussed forty-five minutes," I said. "In fact, I'll set the alarm on my watch."

"No, let's take the full hour, Rachel. We need to talk."

"An hour it is," I said glancing at her hands. The tapping stopped.

Alicia's Role

"I liked the questions you gave me, Rachel. Can we go through them? I wrote some notes." I smiled. "The first one was what do I see as my role? And *why* does TYH have me doing these things? Good questions! I think my role is to be a link

117

between the marketers and the company before the sale and to be a link between the customer and the company after the sale. Why does TYH have someone doing what I'm doing? Because lots of details have to be taken care of to make sure things go right. I mean, sometimes the marketers make a sale, and they don't finish the forms they need to or they might need to find out if there has been a price change. Also, the shipping needs to be considered. You know, the timing and whatever."

"What about the customer and the company part?"

"Well, we need to make the customer happy. Right?"

"Right. So how do you do that?"

"Well, I call the accounting department, confirm the order, provide any information they need, and thank them for their part of the process. If there's any question about the order, the customer usually likes to call me because I have the most information. If they have special needs, I take care of them. Many times the reorders come directly to me."

"I think I know the answer to this question, Alicia, but I'll ask it anyway. Given your role, what part of your work adds the most value?"

"All of it is important, but if you're asking me what I think is most important, it's working with the customer. I wish I had more time to do that. I'd really like to follow up with them and make sure they are happy. I believe we could do a lot more business if I had more time to answer their questions. Sometimes when I talk to them about other products, they increase their orders."

"That leads me to another question. You obviously like to deal with people; you know the products. So why did you turn down the selling job?"

"That's simple. Travel. I won't leave the boys. I'm already gone too much." (Bingo!) So why hadn't she said that to Charlie Rothstein? Because men sometimes don't understand these things, she told me. In response to what she did that she thought was not worth her time, she replied it was TYH follow up and paper work. She was continuously checking with Distribution when orders weren't shipped properly or on time. There were reports she had to file with copies to HR, Distribution and Altis' office, all of which seemed to engender additional questions and requests for more reports. The Marketers were constantly calling in and asking her to make airline reservations, change meetings and clear up questions.

Why wasn't Judy doing that, I wondered. She told me that Judy's predecessor hadn't been very careful about schedules, and everyone came to depend on her. Now that Judy was permanent, she hoped that would change. When I asked her how much of her time was spent on these activities, she told me she didn't know exactly, but they represented frequent interruptions. What was interesting to me is that throughout this discussion so far Alicia had not once looked at her watch, and there had been absolutely no drumming on the table. Nervous energy or stress?

What did she enjoy doing? It was the interactions with the customers. She had a sense that she was good at negotiating deliveries, solving problems and selling products. She was pleased that most people she dealt with regarded her as a friend. What about her aspirations for the next two to three years? She didn't have any. Maybe she would take some time off. (Not good enough I said to myself.) Long term? When the boys were grown, she wanted to be a marketer.

Okay, so now we had some things to talk about. I went back to the early part of the conversation. Do the marketers have laptop computers so they can do some work in processing their own orders? Yes, but they don't use them that way. Accounting prefers to filter the information through one person.

"That may be," I said, "but I'm not sure the option is solely theirs. You spoke of waiting for the boys to grow up—we're talking about years. Would you be satisfied with what you're doing 'til then?"

"Not really. Sometimes I think about leaving. In a way, I'd like to stay home for a while, have another baby. But there are parts of the job I really enjoy."

"Of course, there are. Let's start there. Alicia, if you'll bear with me a minute, I'd like to describe a simple process I use when I move into a job. I think it works just as effectively if you want to transform the job you're in. Want to hear it?"

"Sure, why not?"

Job Transformation: A Process

"The first step is to go through the process we've just been through—determining your role and contribution to the company. There are certain things you enjoy doing because they are personally rewarding. I think of them as fulfilling your purpose. That's the place to start, because when your work and your purpose are in synch, then you get satisfaction from what you're doing."

"So my purpose is working with customers."

"That's the *who*, but my question is *why*?"

"Because I like using my negotiation, problem solving, and selling skills."

"Again. Why?"

"I love helping people solve problems. It gives me a sense that I'm doing something worthwhile."

"And that's why you're so good at it. The next step is to find more time to work on this contribution. *Your strategy, step two, is to look at what you don't enjoy.* In your case, it's taking care of the Marketers' reservations and schedule combined with TYH follow up and reports, answering questions and requests for information from a variety of sources. You've become the hub where requests come and go. No wonder you have so little discretionary time."

"But Rachel, if I like to help people solve problems and make things work, why do I feel the way I do about the Marketers' schedules?"

"Why do you think?"

"Those aren't problems. They're just time killers that any-one could handle. And they take me away from what I re-ally enjoy."

"You're right on target, so let's go to step three. This is where you make an important judgment. *Are all the activities you've de-scribed really necessary?* Take the reports, for example. Do you know how Distribution and HR are using them? Maybe they can be condensed. Perhaps they're just filed. You'd be surprised how often these things become a needless exercise. Someone wants them—just in case.

"Can others do the work better? The answer to that is the next step. For example, are there some things Judy should be do-ing? Perhaps the Marketers should handle their own sched-ules. They've got laptops. Maybe they just need some im-proved software."

"Yes, but they won't like it."

"This is just a *what-if* exercise at this point, Alicia. We're a team, and you're an important member, albeit an overworked one. There are some processes that aren't working as well as they should, and that's a team issue."

"So what's the last step?"

"You take what's left of the work you don't enjoy and figure out how to condense it, develop a program that automates some of it, or find a way to do it better. That might include finding out how oth-ers, highly successful in similar situations, might do the same work. Sometimes we're so close to a situation, it's hard to find creative solutions."

"But how would I do that?"

"I've thought of a way to start, and I'd be willing to help, but since you told me you don't want to travel, it could be a problem."

"Tell me."

"Would Tomás let you go out of town for a couple of days, I mean if it weren't a routine situation?"

"I think so, especially if it meant that I'd be happier at work. He's a very good husband."

"Well, then, I know someone at Perry Winkle Enterprises who is great at streamlining activities and examining work processes. I think he could show you around and offer some help. And there's another person there, a computer genius, who might offer some automation solutions."

"Could I really go?"

"Of course, you could. Next week, if you'd like."

"Let me talk to Tomás first."

"Okay, you let me know when you can go, and I'll make the contacts. Sound okay?"

"How long would I be gone?"

"Two or three days at the most, but I promise you, it'll be worth it. Can you talk to Tomás this weekend and let me know Monday?"

"I will. Rachel. You don't know how much I appreciate your help. Why are you doing this for me?"

"I like you, Alicia, I really do. And besides, you're too valuable to hide behind stacks and stacks of reports. One more question, okay?"

"I tried, Rachel. I mean it. Maybe I'm not so good at giving feedback, but Katy's got such a temper when she gets riled up. I tried a couple of times, I really did."

"Thanks, Alicia. I understand completely. Still, situations like yours and Katy's have to be settled at some point. Right?"

"Right." She looked at her watch and back at me. "Thank you," she said and went back to her office.

So that's where we left things. She had her Katy; I had my Stuart. Talk about common ground!

Clarifying a Person's Thinking about Her Current Role

Many times, mentoring issues directly relate to the person's dissatisfaction with work. By the effective use of good questions, you can help someone clarify her thinking about this. The first step is to help the person think through the essential elements of the job, including:

➢ The purpose of the job, why it exists. If necessary, ask questions to help the person differentiate between the job (actual work done) and the role (why it needs to be done).

➢ What part of the work contributes the most role value?

Transforming the Job

➢ Help the mentee identify the area in which she makes the greatest contribution and obtains the greatest satisfaction.

➢ What part constitutes the area of least contribution? Are all these activities really necessary?

➢ Should someone else be doing these activities? Or can someone do them more effectively?

➢ Is there a way to streamline the work?

The idea behind these questions is to help the individual find more discretionary time to pursue greater contribution by enhancing her role, pursuing learning opportunities or focusing more attention on the areas of work that produce the greatest satisfaction.

CHAPTER 9
Straight Talk

The greatest discovery of my generation is that human beings, by changing the inner attitudes of their minds, can change the outer aspects of their lives. It is too bad that more people will not accept this tremendous discovery and begin living it.

— William James

When I got back to my office, I found an e-mail from Judy. The votes had been tallied, and I was not surprised to see that almost everyone, with the exception of Judy, had opted to make individual art work choices. Katy had suggested a team meeting to discuss next steps, and Judy, after checking everyone's calendars, had set it for three today. Fast work! I stopped by Judy's desk and asked her to invite Justin. While official announcements weren't out yet, I thought it would be a good time to introduce him to the team, and I certainly didn't want him to miss getting the information about the walls. Lily had assured me there would be an e-mail announcement about the transfer by four today.

A few minutes before three, Justin came by my office, and we walked together to the conference room. With everyone assembled, I welcomed him officially to Marketing. Everyone knew Justin because TYH was a small company, but I could tell his moving into the group surprised Katy and Stuart, who were exchanging sidelong glances. On the other hand, Alicia said she was very pleased with the choice since she had worked with Justin several times before on project teams.

We all sat at the conference table, that is, everyone but Katy. She had placed a flip chart pad and markers near the end of the table and immediately took charge. "Judy and I went to look at the warehouse pictures," she said with a nod toward Judy. "They're just not suitable. Rachel has the name of a woman who owns a frame shop, and she will be here Monday, find out what we want, and work with each of us individually to select the pictures for our walls. There is approximately $6,000 available," she said, writing large red numbers on the flip chart, "and that makes about $850.00 apiece," she added, sounding very much like my third grade math teacher.

"I've got a question," said Alicia. "There's a new art store near my house. I'd like to take a look over there and see if I can find something that I like."

"I have a friend who's an artist," said Justin. "Would it be possible to buy one of his paintings?"

"But it's already been decided," said Katy.

"Eight hundred and fifty dollars. Are you kidding?" said Stuart. "That'll buy one picture."

Tom Gaines guffawed. "Come on, Kennedy. Is Prince Charles dropping by for tea?"

"This is my meeting," said Katy, "so quiet down and let me finish, please."

Everyone got quiet. All of a sudden, all eyes were fixed on the commanding symbol of authority standing before them with flashing eyes. Surprisingly, Alicia was the first to speak. "Sit down, Katy. I don't think this is *your* meeting," she said, her face flushed in anger. "This is for all of us, isn't it Rachel?"

I nodded.

For a moment, Katy hesitated. Then she sat down. Stuart immediately jumped in. "Don't go off the deep end, Alicia. That's not what she meant."

"I'm not going off the deep end," said Alicia, with a previously unheard (at least by me) edge in her voice. "I don't like being talked down to." All of a sudden, everyone was talking at once.

"Simmer down—please." That was Tom, the voice of reason. "Katy, my friend, you're out of line."

"So are you," said Stuart.

"One moment," I said. It was time, and I knew it. "Let's stop action, take deep breaths and talk about what's going on here."

Judy was shaking her head. "This was meant to be such a positive meeting."

"So what happened?" I asked.

"We blew it," said Judy. "Katy, I think you took over, and...."

"I know," said Katy in her best drill sergeant voice, "but we agreed that since *I* called the meeting and *I* had the agenda, it was my meeting—and then everyone started talking at once, and no one wanted to listen."

"Who agreed?" I wondered.

"Everyone—Judy and me," Katy replied, her voice beginning to waver.

"What else do we need to talk about?" said Stuart, changing the subject. "I'm ready to get back to *Rachel's* big decoration project." I let that pass. This was not the moment to have it out with him.

I polled the group. No one wanted to continue discussing what had happened in the meeting. Things quieted down considerably after that. Judy suggested, and the group agreed, that everyone would meet with Marie from the Frame Shop on Monday. Those who wanted to shop somewhere else over the weekend could do that. If anyone wanted to go to the Frame Shop and select pictures over the weekend, that would be fine too.

Following the meeting, I went back to my office. "Rachel, could I talk to you?" It was a very subdued Katy.

"Come on in," I said, "and close the door, if you like."

Katy Gets the Message

She stepped inside, and I saw the beginnings of tears pooling in her eyes. "Look, I blew it today and I know it."

"Sit down and let's talk about it," I said coming around my desk and sitting in one of the overstuffed chairs. She sat in the other and for a few moments said nothing. I did not break the silence because I hoped that Katy was thinking about the impact of her actions today, and I wanted to do nothing to reduce the value of her insights.

Usually so articulate, she was struggling for the right words. "I made a fool of myself. Everyone was talking at once and I wanted, I wanted to..." She reached into her pocket for a tissue.

I resisted responding, but I leaned forward in my chair to show her I was listening.

She dabbed at her eyes. "I wanted them to listen, but it came out all wrong. I sounded like a junior high school teacher shushing a bunch of misbehaving kids. I knew it the minute I looked at their faces. I really offended Alicia, and Justin looked like he wanted to go back to Human Resources. What a mess! Now everyone thinks I'm out of control. Even Tom, Mr. Nice Guy, said I was wrong. I had a big falling out with Alicia a few days ago, Rachel, and I mishandled that too—just like the Super Health situation with Frank Manchester. I don't think she has any respect for me anymore, and I don't blame her. What am I going to do?" A fresh supply of tears filled her eyes.

I waited for a moment because I wanted her to say everything she needed to say. This was a very important moment for Katy, much more significant than if Alicia had given her private feedback. There was a message for her, and I was sure she received it.

Straight Talk with Katy

"I'm not going to give you a bunch of platitudes," I said finally, "but I want to help. This isn't the end of the world or of your reputation either. You're good, Katy. You've got all the makings of a superstar. Today, as you said, you blew it. So now, you've got an opportunity, and I have a hunch you'll handle that like a superstar."

"I guess I should apologize to everyone, is that it?"

"I don't think it would hurt. At the same time, you've learned something about the skills you need to acquire in order to deal with conflict more effectively. The important question is, how can you acquire or strengthen these skills?"

"I guess I could use some training, don't you think so, Rachel?"

"It seems to me, it would be helpful to sign up for training. You'd have the opportunity to practice, do some role plays, and get feedback."

"But right now, what do you think are the most important things for me to learn? I liked what you told me about apologizing. I just wish I didn't have to use it so often. Are there some rules about conflict that would help me?"

"I've tried to learn from my own experience, Katy. I used to 'fly off the handle' when I was faced with conflict situations. In fact, in the early part of my career, I spent a good bit of time explaining 'what I really meant' and apologizing for things I wish I hadn't said. (Elroy Grant used to call that 'tap dancing backwards.') One day, like you, I decided there must be an easier way to handle things. My insight came as a result of a meeting where I argued my way to success, or so I thought, until Elroy opened my eyes. He said the next time people would be on their guard with me. But when I changed my style, I learned that mistakes aren't fatal. They're just wake up calls. So here's a few ideas that have helped me both in business and in my personal life. Some I've learned from experience, mine and that of others. Some I've learned through training.

Handling Conflict Situations

"Conflict is very natural. It occurs when someone else's values, beliefs, interests, or opinions stand in the way of what I need or want. Putting it that way helps me look at the situation rationally instead of from the perspective of my feelings. I've learned that whenever I tie things up with my feelings, I lose my objectivity and my edge when it comes to problem-solving."

"I guess I wasn't feeling too objective in there," said Katy.

"Probably not. What helps me is that before I get involved in any conflict situation, I ask myself three questions:

Does it really matter? I don't know about you, Katy, but I've seen people work themselves into a frenzy over the smallest, most unimportant things. They say during the Christmas season, for example, people become ruder, more aggressive, and more likely to take it out on others just because they have to stand in line a few minutes more than usual or wait for an extra light at intersections. Think of the energy and good spirits wasted on these minor annoyances." She nodded waiting for me to continue.

Is it worthy of me? Arguing about who is right in most instances isn't productive and usually doesn't make much difference. In the end, that's not the me that I'm trying to project, and finally,

Will this achieve the best outcome? Suppose I'm angry, I call and I tell you what I think. The question is, what have

I gained? Probably, you won't forget what I said, even when we finally get the matter resolved. Someone once told me you can tell how wise a person is by his attitude toward time. A foolish person makes decisions based on how he feels today. A wise person asks himself, how will this affect eternity?"

"I guess I didn't gain much in the meeting. And now everyone will remember what happened."

"That's true. However, the most important thing isn't what happened but what *you take away from it*. I don't want you to think for a moment that I go through this process perfectly every time. Sometimes, I get angry before I really think things through. What I am describing are my aspirations."

"I can understand that, Rachel. I mean, it's a rational way of looking at things, but sometimes I just feel the anger or frustration welling up in me."

"Of course, you do. So do I. *The question isn't how you feel, but rather what you do about it*. That's what counts. If you find yourself feeling angry a lot, it helps to go back and see what triggers those feelings. Is it frustration? Is it stress? Is it needing to be right? Do you get annoyed when people waste your time or disagree with you? When you find yourself in one of these situations, it helps to make a few notes so you can look for patterns. Once you become conscious of the triggers, you can manage your response by changing the way you think about these things. That's called *reframing*.

"Another thing that works for me," I continued, "is to compare the situation on a scale of one to ten to something that is really horrible. Then I can dismiss what's going on by realizing how small it is in relation to things that count. These strategies work, and they are easy to do; the key is awareness. So, that's why it's important to understand where your greatest challenges lie. For me, it's dealing with people who are arrogant or sarcastic. When I see someone with an attitude I think of as destructive, I want to lash out, but isn't that being judgmental and arrogant too? You see, I've learned that getting angry often produces the opposite effect of what I'm trying to achieve."

"Me too, but it's not attitude that gets to me. In the case of Super Health, I was frustrated by their inept way of handling things. I felt that I shouldn't have to waste my time dealing with their lack of efficiency. With Alicia, I just thought she should have talked to me if she had a problem with what I did. I guess at the meeting today, I was frustrated. They were acting like a bunch of whiny school kids."

"Maybe people were reacting to being pushed," I said. "This whole 'wall thing' has been fraught with emotion from the beginning, and today was an expression of it. I thought it was pretty healthy, but it must have felt uncomfortable from where you were."

"I wish I had your insight," said Katy.

"Don't put too much relevance on the fact that I see this situation logically," I told her. "After all, it's easier for me because I'm not emotionally involved in it. Just remember, in most situations there's more than one way to arrive at a good answer. I try to remember this when someone has a different idea on how to handle things. If I want others to listen to me, I first must be willing to hear what they think, without interrupting, being defensive or arguing."

"I guess I can get pretty defensive sometimes," said Katy.

"I think you do, sometimes. It helps to be aware of it, and, if you want to do something about it, there's some good resources you can use. One source book for discourse is Ben Franklin's *Autobiography*. In it he says he made a practice of avoiding dogmatic language. He pointed out that by doing so, he found others more willing to hear his views, and he also felt it was easier to back down if he was wrong."

"I suppose I should read that book. But what did he mean by *dogmatic* language?"

"He was talking about assertions like '*I know*,' '*I'm certain*,' '*I'm right*,' and '*you're wrong*.' Instead, he substituted softeners like *'It seems to me,'* *'In my opinion,'* and *'I think at this time.'* Franklin was one of the great diplomats of all time, and if he made that a rule, it means he fell short of it from time to time himself. See, Katy, you and I are in good company."

Katy smiled. "But aren't there people you have personality conflicts with? I mean, everyone likes some people better than others. And I find some people almost annoying. Do you know what I mean?"

"For sure. But, Katy, this is business. If someone wanted to spend a million dollars with us, wouldn't you overlook those annoyances?" She nodded.

"If you can do that, then you can overlook the minor annoyances you might have with co-workers. So often, the behavior of others is a mirror of our attitude toward them. What helps me is to decide, for my own peace of mind, that everyone is doing the best he can. I've found that when I treat someone like a million dollar customer, he tends to treat me better as well. It also turns out that I feel better. The funny part of personality conflicts is they rob us of energy. When it comes to problems, personality or otherwise, I go back to those first three questions: Does it matter? Is it worthy of me? And what will the outcome be?"

"Maybe so...I guess you're right, but I can't always help the way I feel."

The Fallacy of Focusing on Feelings

"I know. Neither can I. At the same time, Katy, what I've found, at least in my own case is, *it's best not to focus on how I feel. What I do* is far more important. If I worry about what's going on with the other person, I'm literally working 'the wrong side of the street.' I remember years ago that I had a conflict with a co-worker. Her office was three doors down the hall, but you would have thought we were miles away from one another. She used to write me long memos criticizing my part of a brochure that we were supposed to be working on together. I don't know how much energy I wasted fuming about that."

"So what did you do?"

"Instead of confronting her, I complained to my boss. Needless to say, he didn't want to hear about it. He said he had his share of problems and told me he had great confidence in my ability to solve my own. He also gave me a piece of advice which I follow to this day. He said, 'Rachel, forget about who's right or wrong. It's important to know that when you come to me and complain about someone else, it makes you look weak. If you can't resolve a simple personal problem, how can I ask you to work on larger, more complex issues?'"

Handling "Sabotage"

"I never thought about that, Rachel. But what if the person is sabotaging you?"

"Sabotaging?"

"Suppose someone goes behind your back and talks about you to someone else, and you find out about it? What should you do?"

"It depends on the situation. I mean, even if we think someone is sabotaging us, the best way to deal with it is to be straightforward. Otherwise, these concerns become a distraction. Decide on the outcome you want and work from there. Understand this, *there's no way we can control anyone but ourselves. What we think and how we act are always up to us.* Would taking action help? If so, tell that person what you've heard. By confronting the person, you do two things: put her on notice that you are aware of the problem and give her a chance to respond. Expect a defensive reaction and a denial. Then cut through the defensiveness by saying, 'I'd like to work things out because I'm very interested in our having a good working relationship.' Find out how the other person feels about that. *Look for areas of agreement.* Then you can problem solve. We can change our mental state by focusing on a good resolution and by leaving the judging side to someone else. You don't have to *like* everyone. The most important thing is to approach the other person in an open, courteous and rational way. And be careful, Katy, when you apply terms like *sabotage*, you've already injected an emotional component, and that may not be in your best interests."

"One more question, Rachel. What if, in spite of all the things you try, things still don't get better? Then what do you do?"

"That's when you bring in a third party, someone with experience in helping people resolve sticky situations."

"Someone like you, I'll bet."

"Thanks for saying that. Yes, someone like me. It's a good strategy when you've reached an impasse. Someone who is objective can generally set some boundaries and help both parties talk about their needs and wants. That's probably more advice than you can use right now, Katy. It's a subject I like to talk about, and I hope I haven't overdone it."

"It's good advice, Rachel, and I'm going to think about everything you said. I feel better already. I think I'm going to talk to Alicia in the next day or so. Right now, I'm not ready, but when I am, I hope she will be willing to listen."

"Do you think it might help if you checked with her as to when would be a good time?"

"I think it would. She's always so busy. And she does so much for all of us."

"It wouldn't hurt to tell her so. And Katy, any time I can help you or you just want to talk, my door is open. I meant it when I said you've got the makings of a superstar. Next week I'd like to carve out some time to consider how best to assure that happens here at TYH."

"I'd like that," Katy said softly. She went to the door, opened it and turned back toward me. "I almost forgot to tell you, I goofed today, and I'm really sorry. Is there anything I can do?"

"You've already done it."

"Then, thank you for your help."

"You're welcome."

```
To: egrant@pwe.net
From: Rachel@pwe.net
```

Today's meeting might have worked a minor
miracle. A small bloodletting based on
pent-up frustrations about autocratic management. Katy "got it" in more ways than
one. Acting as self-anointed leader, she
finally heard some direct, on-the-spot
feedback. Afterwards, we talked. I really
feel positive about her willingness to
learn from what happened. Group moving
toward more self-direction. Stay tuned.

Rachel

```
To: Rachel@pwe.net
From: egrant@pwe.net
```

Great news! Sounds like you're on track.
Let's try to keep Ms. Stanford graduate on
the payroll. She sounds like a future asset
to me. Did I miss something? I saw no mention of your talk with Kennedy. On the
agenda for next week? Have a great weekend.

Elroy

Responding vs. Reacting

I knew I needed to talk with Stuart and soon. We both stood
to profit from a better working relationship, even in the short
term, but it was a difficult situation, and I was avoiding it. What
I needed to resolve was how to get through the barriers of his
cynicism and my reaction to it. I reminded myself that in a conflict situation, it is extremely important to *respond* rather than
react. When I respond, I am powerful because I have engaged
my rational, thinking self. When I react, I am weakened because
I'm focusing on my emotions.

What I needed to remember was that feeling a strong need to react is always a red flag. It tells me I need to disengage immediately. (The way I do this is to change my perspective *physically* by moving away or looking somewhere else, or *emotionally* by pausing and taking a few deep breaths.)

I also know that my body language reveals what I'm thinking, so I need to make sure it doesn't conflict with the message I'm trying to send.

Body language! Tom had told me my shoulders were up to my ears the last time I met with Stuart. I wonder what my face had revealed. I would do better next time, and I would meet with him soon.

But that night, when I finally went to sleep, my concerns persisted. I dreamed I was running in a dark alley. There was a shadowy figure of a man, and I was chasing him. He was only a few feet ahead of me, but the ground was rocky, and I couldn't increase my pace because I didn't want to fall. I looked behind me and there was a big grizzly bear nipping at my heels.

❋   ❋   ❋

Saturday morning was filled with expectation. Shortly after ten I got a call from security, and minutes later Paul was at the door. "Coffee on?" he asked holding up a bag of bagels he had bought at the airport. We spoke briefly about our adult child. Paul said he was fine and that he was glad he'd be gainfully employed, if only for a month or two. Both of us realized that slicing tomatoes and serving fries did not represent our best hopes for Brad's future. It was a major surprise that he hadn't seen it himself.

The rest of the weekend went by too swiftly. Saturday afternoon, I introduced Paul to Lucien and Beth. That night the four of us experienced a superb Chinese dinner at North China Restaurant, an elegant but quiet place where we could enjoy each other's company. Sunday came too soon, and around two o'clock, Paul left for Oakville.

I know there were times when we seemed to forget the sacrifices you made to come to Houston all alone, far away from your family and friends. And you must have thought we were oblivious to the good things you were trying to do for us.

How true that was of Monday. Everything started out fine. First thing in the morning, Alicia stopped by to tell me Tomás had agreed to let her make the trip to Oakville. The timing was strictly up to me, and if it could be arranged, she could go next week. I promised to make some phone calls and let the people who would be meeting with her know they could expect her call within the next few days. Arrangements would be up to them.

Shortly after ten Marie, Beth's friend who owned and managed the Frame Shop, stopped by my office briefly and assured me that $850 would buy several pictures for each office. She had brought framed pictures, prints and catalogs so every person would have many pictures from which to choose. My office was to be the last on her rounds. At noon Judy knocked on my door and told me Marie was ready for me. Paul and I travel frequently to tropical islands, so I chose beach scenes to remind me of Caribbean vacations, hoping that the person who replaced me wasn't a skier. No matter, I felt someone at TYH would be delighted to cover the empty spaces with blue horizons, golden beaches, and skies full of birds.

Everyone, said Marie, had been very pleased with the pictures and had stayed well within the budget, that is everyone except Stuart, who had managed to select $1,300 worth of pictures. There were a few dollars left over, and I realized that it would be possible to do this, but somehow it didn't seem right. Besides, based on the way he had acted in the meeting Friday, I suspected this had less to do with overrunning the picture budget than it had to do with Mr. Kennedy making another statement. One thing was for sure, there would be no more procrastination for me. I was getting tired of playing games, and I knew it was time for us to talk.

Straight Talk with Stuart

Once again, I decided to do some planning first, even though I was keenly aware it hadn't helped before. This time I decided more than anything, I would focus on the outcome. I had no illusions that Stuart would welcome what I had to say, but there were two things I was sure of: at the end of our conversation, (1) he would understand that whatever happened to him from this point on was strictly his decision, and (2) he would know I was ready to help him, but only if he asked for my help. With these two thoughts in mind, I headed for his office.

He was talking on the phone and pacing, his back toward the door. "I don't know what happened, Robert, but be sure I'm going to find out," he said and turning in my direction seemed startled to see me. "I'll call you back," he said hurriedly hanging up the phone.

"Would you prefer me to come back in ten or fifteen minutes?" I asked.

"No," he responded, looking at me quizzically. "Let's talk now."

"About the pictures," I began. "Marie tells me you went quite a bit beyond the budget. Obviously, that creates a bit of a problem."

"I'll handle it," he said. "I just thought that maybe you'd have enough pull to spend a little extra and get people what they really wanted."

He paused, waiting to see if I'd take the bait. I didn't. After what seemed like a long silence, he continued, "It isn't nearly enough money, but I'll just have to settle for one picture," he said. "I guess you tried, and it was the best you could do."

"I didn't get the impression anyone else was particularly concerned about it."

"Of course, you didn't. Why would you? And while we're talking, could you tell me why you're bringing in Justin Graves over Robert Darman, who just happens to be three times more qualified?"

"It was a close call," I said.

"Excuse me! Close? I don't see how! None of the marketing managers I've known would have picked someone with no marketing education or background when he had a good candidate who had both."

I took a few deep breaths. "Just so you'll know, I consulted with several people in whom I have great confidence. It's not that Robert wasn't a strong contender but that Justin was also one and for different reasons. In the end, it was my decision, and I guess that's all I'm willing to say about the subject. So, thanks for asking, but case closed."

"Case closed?" His jaw was tensed, his neck flecked with small red spots.

"I'm wondering Stuart, what have I done to make you so angry?"

"I don't know what you're talking about. I'm not angry—not at all."

"Well, perhaps I've come to the wrong conclusion, but it's based on your tone, your comments and the fact that your fists are clenched."

"Okay, so I'm not particularly happy right now. Look, this is nothing against you personally so don't take it that way. I'm sure you're *trying* your best. But why didn't they send someone who knows something about this business?"

I had made up my mind that nothing Stuart said was going to make me lose my composure, so I took another deep breath and responded, "That's a good question. The truth is that Elroy Grant sent me here to assess the situation and see what I could do to help everyone, but I'm stuck when it comes to you, Stuart.

I've been told you have leadership ability, but I have yet to see you using it. The focus of your energy appears to be on tearing things down rather than on being the achiever I've heard you are. That puzzles me because you've told me you'd like to move up."

"I don't know what you're talking about, Rachel. Can you *try* to be more specific?" he said in a tone that confirmed all that I had already said.

"For one thing, Stuart, please stop using the word *try* when it comes to me. Honestly, I find it demeaning. I'll be glad to be more specific. In every encounter we've had, including this one, there's been a caustic undertone. I want to work with you and help in any way I can, but I'm really finding it difficult. Any suggestions?"

"No," he said.

"Then, let me make one. *You're at a critical moment in your TYH career.* The most important thing for you to think about is your future."

"What do you mean?"

"I've heard you're very talented, but you are damaging your reputation with your cynicism. You might want to step back and look at what's happened. Your co-workers and supervisors have seen it. I've certainly been aware of it in our two previous discussions and in Friday's meeting. Today's handling of the pictures is just another example." I paused to see if he wanted to say something. He didn't. "Stuart, it's not too late. Things probably haven't worked out to be what you expected—but that happens to a lot of people, and they pick up and go on. You've got options to consider, but if your attitude doesn't improve, they'll be more and more limited. The decision of what happens to your career is in your hands. I've offered to help, but..."

"What can *you* do for me?"

"Not one thing until you decide you want help. It's up to you, Stuart. Is there anything you want to talk about?"

"Yes, you said Elroy Grant was coming. Can you tell me when?"

"Not precisely but it'll be in the next couple of weeks."

"Have you spoken to him about me?"

"I've spoken to Elroy about everyone." I paused to let that news sink in. It did. "Is there anything more?"

"I don't think so. I guess I'll think about my options. As you said, it's my choice."

"Right, and I'm available to talk. Anytime."

He turned toward his desk. "I've got some things to do right now." I nodded, said an unanswered goodbye and left.

```
To: egrant@pwe.net
From: Rachel@pwe.net

   I talked with Stuart today. Don't ask me
   how it went, because I'm not sure. He had
   little to say except for questioning my
   competence. Suffice it to say, I've deliv-
   ered the message of choice, responsibility
   and options. The next step is his.

   Rachel
```

Several hours later:

```
To: Rachel@pwe.net
From: egrant@pwe.net

   Good work. All injections hurt going in.
   The question is, will the medicine take
   effect or is the patient beyond help. Time
   will tell.

   Elroy

   P.S. You're the most competent person I
   know.
```

Elroy had a genius for saying the right thing.

NOTES TO MENTORING FILE

The Mentor as Honest and Empathetic Listener

If you're faced with mentoring someone past a powerful, emotional experience, it's important to let the person tell you the "whole story" in his own words. Resist the urge to underplay or overplay the situation. And don't try to make things better. Sometimes learning something is painful, but it's a growth experience. This is one time when you should try VERY HARD to share a similar situation. Make your story short. The important message is, you didn't die, and you weren't fired. A very effective comment a mentor once made to me in such a situation was: "Let's go to school on this one." I immediately realized I was in a learning mode. That's what you want to help the mentee see.

Before engaging in a conflict, ask these boundary questions:

1. Does this really matter to me?

2. Is it worthy of me?

3. If I engage, will it achieve the best outcome?

When problem solving with others, use this three-step approach:

1. First agree on the *desired outcome*. That's critical. Unless both want the same result, there's no way to settle differences on how to get there.

2. Before discussing disagreements, emphasize *areas* of agreement.

3. Negotiate to solve the differences.

Responding Rather Than Reacting
in Conflict Situations

Responding is a more powerful way of handling things because it engages your thinking process. Reacting focuses on emotions. A strong reaction is a red flag. You should immediately disengage in these ways:

1. Change perspective *physically* by moving away or looking somewhere else.

2. Change perspective *emotionally* by pausing and taking a few deep breaths.

3. If neither approach works, make whatever excuse is necessary to take a break from the action.

CHAPTER 10
Building Confidence

Everything happens to everyone sooner or later if there is time enough.

— George Bernard Shaw

Tuesday and Wednesday were uneventful. After Monday, they seemed almost like the intermission in a melodrama. There was still much to do, but thank goodness, no tragedies involved. Tuesday, I made calls to two PWE work processes superstars, and they were delighted that Alicia was coming to visit. She would be calling sometime today or early tomorrow I told them. My third call was to Elroy, who said he would have his secretary handle logistics, hotel arrangements, and morning pickups, organize a small dinner meeting on Alicia's first night, and if he were available, he would personally handle her PWE tour. She was slated for the royal treatment. "If you send her here, that's good enough for me," he said. When I told Alicia how things were going, you would have thought I'd doubled her salary. I couldn't think of anyone more deserving, and if everything went as I expected, that rock she was pushing uphill would soon be history. No mention was made of a discussion with Katy, and I decided not to ask.

When I learned Katy was out Wednesday, having called in with a stomach virus, I had a sharp attack of anxiety thinking back to my first meeting with the Marketers. Gayle had been out with a "stomach virus" too, and I couldn't help remembering she had been interviewing for another job. No, I decided, I'm not going to be paranoid. People do actually get sick from time to time. I must admit, I felt better when Judy said Katy was on the phone and wanted to speak to me. Her voice sounded weak as she told me she had been up all night with stomach problems. "I'll be in tomorrow, if I live," she told me.

"Hurry up, and get well. We all miss you," I responded. "But don't come back until you really feel better." I laughed later as I thought about my feeling healthy and celebrating Katy's illness. "She is sick. Hooray!" Ah, Rachel, I thought, you're the sick one here.

Shortly after that Justin arrived carrying cardboard boxes of his personal belongings from his other office. He parked them outside my door when I invited him in for a chat. I enjoyed the hour we spent getting better acquainted. In fact, the more I talked to Justin Graves, the more convinced I was that he was ready for the Marketing job. He was high on To Your Health products, liked working for the company, and looked forward to the challenge. I couldn't help thinking he was just the opposite of Stuart, and wondering if Stuart had once been as bright-eyed and eager. It was this thought that kept me hoping we could salvage what had once been a promising young man with great career prospects. I tried to call Tom to let him know Justin had arrived but learned from Judy he was visiting customers in the Houston area. Justin had some leftover work from HR plus the chore of moving into his new office, so for now, the welcome peace continued within the TYH Marketing organization.

When Tom called to see what was going on, Judy asked if I wanted to talk with him. I did. I was wondering about the progress on the potential visits to out of town customers that we had discussed. Was that still on? Had Tom talked with Stuart yet? Or Katy? Tom told me they were getting together Friday. He had waited until Justin was officially in the group so he could be there. I asked him as a favor to include Alicia. While she was not technically a part of sales, she was a big contributor. He thanked me and said she would definitely be invited. So far as I knew, only Judy and I were not, but that was what I wanted.

Friday morning the pictures arrived. Marie had brought a two-person crew to hang them, so little work was accomplished as our small group walked from office to office watching the transformation and in the process discovering some interesting facts about each other. A less-exuberant Katy had returned this morning professing to be much better and was part of the entourage. Judy combined listening for the telephones with squeezing in a few scattered moments to walk into each office and admire the work in progress. Although Tom and Justin were engrossed in conversation, they moved along with the rest of us. Stuart was in his office but notably absent from the group.

What fascinated us was learning about each other from the pictures we had chosen. My beach scenes led Alicia to ask which islands Paul and I had visited. Tom preferred St. Thomas to Bermuda, but Katy disagreed, citing the preferences of a friend who had sailed to both islands. The sailing pictures in her office led to some good-natured laughter and nosy questions about her love life. Stuart had selected a collage of golf courses, actually grinning when Katy asked how many Mulligans he usually took and scoffed at his denial. I admired the picture but said little beyond that for Stuart avoided my glances. Alicia's scenes of Mediterranean architecture on the edge of deep blue waters reflected the house she wanted to live in someday. Floral

146

bouquets decorated Judy's walls, and we discovered she grew African violets indoors and prize-winning roses outside. Justin's mountains were a far cry from Houston's flat terrain, but he assured us he saw plenty of them each year during the skiing season. Tom pointed out that with the new baby, it might be several years before he saw them again. Justin refused to rise to the bait and just smiled. Tom's pictures of hunting dogs and birds reflected a favorite pastime. "Rachel, if you don't see me around during duck season," he said, "it's because I'm showing our customers why they need TYH vitamins."

Judy took me aside. "You and Katy were right," she said, "it would have been a shame to pick a theme when all of us really had our own ideas about what we enjoy."

"I think we did pick a theme, Judy. It was self-expression. Maybe a bit broad, but the place looks so much better."

It did. And then we found a surprise waiting for us. Marie had brought two pictures for the small conference room. "I'd like to throw these in," she said, "compliments of me and two of your greatest admirers: Lucien and Beth." They were warm-colored landscapes, small cottages, trees, and country lanes. "I can't...."

"Of course you can," she said. "If you don't like them, I can go back and get some others."

"I love them." I turned toward the group and asked, "In or out?"

Tom's thumbs up signal was followed by a host of similar gestures, so it was agreed.

Challenging the Status Quo

By noon, Marie and her crew had disappeared. When I returned from lunch, there was a pink slip bearing a telephone message on my desk from Lily Sheldon, HR Manager, who asked that I return the call ASAP. Was it about Justin, or perhaps a question from Robert? No, it wasn't. She understood that I had someone here this morning putting pictures on the wall. Was that right? Yes, I said, that's right. Would she like to come down this afternoon and see for herself? She would, and she did.

Within fifteen minutes I heard her in Judy's reception area. She had brought reinforcements, an afternoon visit from the picture police. There were three people in all. Lily introduced me to the Assistant HR Manager, Sheldon Cosgrove, and the Building Manager, J. Paxton, heavy hitters all. I wondered silently if they didn't have far more important matters to attend to, but I knew this was a key political moment, and I could not act as if I took it lightly. One piece of wisdom I have learned over the years—no matter how amused one might be at an organization's bureaucratic behavior, one must behave as if it is a matter of the utmost importance, and so I did.

We moved from one office to another, with me doing most of the talking. As I conducted the tour, I noticed how their eyes moved from the pictures to each other in a wordless conspiratorial dialogue, and I wondered what they were thinking. Little was said beyond, "Oh, now that's interesting," or an inquiry, "So whose office is this, Rachel?" At the end of the tour we walked into the conference room and Lily sat down. So did the others. It was time for the inquisition.

Lily admitted the offices looked very business-like but wondered if I was aware of the "situation with the walls," and particularly that Altis had asked her to approve all pictures. I said I heard there was a process like that several years ago but thought it had probably expired by now. "Who told you that?" Lily wondered, pursing her lips. I changed the subject, apologizing if I had violated any company rules. Did she want us to take them all down? "No," she responded with a weak smile. Actually she thought they looked rather nice but cautioned me about any further straying from the rules. She turned to the other two and they nodded their heads in unison. I thanked them for coming by, wished them a great weekend, and they departed to attend to other important matters.

Before the end of the day, several people from Accounting had wandered by. No sooner had they left than I got a call from Ron Corbin, the Assistant Controller who had advised me about the money available for the project. He said he heard that our offices looked great and asked for the name and number of the art gallery and frame shop that had done the work. Drop a pebble into a still pond and just watch the ripples.

* * *

Saturday morning I caught a plane back to Pembroke. Traveling was tough, but being away from Paul and Brad was much harder. On the way home from the airport, Paul brought me up to date on the saga of our young entrepreneur. He'd been at work less than a week, but his education curve was moving straight up. It was amazing what a resourceful young management trainee can learn after just a few days in captivity. His new found knowledge amounted to (1) customers can be very hard to please, (2) he didn't want to spend the next six months cleaning restrooms, and (3) filling in for other people can wreak havoc on your love life. It seems that one person didn't show up for work Friday night. Brad had to cancel a date with Nikki, and she was not happy.

I was jubilant. Maybe this spelled the end of a promising career. I wondered if he was home, and Paul said he was and wanted to talk to us. My heart leaped up. Perhaps he was ready to go back to school. Paul put his arm around my shoulder. "Don't depend on it," he said. "It's going to take more than a week in the gulag for Brad to get the message."

He was in his room when I arrived, getting ready for a tennis game. Billy and Chula gave me a high profile Chihuahua-style welcome, and Brad hugged me. "Back from the wars, Mom?" he asked.

"Just a little R and R," I responded with a smile. "I've missed you."

"Me too."

"How's the job?"

He signaled "so, so" with his right hand adding verbally, "I'll have it wired in a few days. We just need to get personnel straightened out so I can quit the routine with yucky bathrooms. And they're going to have to be more dependable too. Nikki says she won't be so forgiving next time. I'm learning lots about management," he added.

"Oh?"

"People can be hard to please, but if you smile a lot, they generally act better. We've got a few Grumpy Gusses on the cash registers. I'm going to work on them."

"Good for you. And what will happen if they don't reform?"

"They will. But that's not what I wanted to talk with you and Dad about."

We looked at him expectantly.

Leaving Home

"Now don't throw a fit, Mom, Dad." I took a few deep breaths. "Pete Redfield and I want to move in together. Before you say 'no' let me tell you about it. It's a small apartment above a garage just a couple of miles from here. It has one bedroom and room for a fold out couch in the living room, and it won't cost much. They're paying for gas and electricity."

I was silent. Paul spoke up. "When do you plan to move?" he asked.

"Monday, but..." I had a picture of furniture being moved in, lights on, telephone installed. Sounded like a relaxing weekend.

"But?" That was Paul.

"I hate to ask, but I could use a little help."

"Help?" That was me.

"We have to put up two months rent, put a deposit down for a telephone, and get a few essentials." Essentials turned out to be furniture, groceries, towels, and all those things it takes to start up a household.

"Are you sure you want to do this, son?" asked Paul. "That could mean staying in this job for some time." That prospect alone would have been enough to change my mind.

"I'm positive, Dad. It's time I got out on my own. I guess I'm going to need about $500, but I'll pay it back. I promise."

Who could resist? Brad had known Pete since kindergarten. He informed us Pete was still attending Pembroke, the college from which Brad had so recently departed. Maybe he would influence our son to go back to school. There was another piece of good news. The apartment turned out to be behind a duplex owned by Robert Montoya, the director of Pembroke's little theater. Montoya, a smart business man and a long time acquaintance, had agreed to let the boys move their furniture in over the weekend. He and his wife lived in one of the duplexes and two male college students leased the other. More good news. Being around college students might rub off on Brad. So I put my concerns aside, and Paul and I spent much of the weekend shopping with Brad and Pete.

At first they insisted on shopping at Stanley's, Oakville's largest furniture store, but once they saw the prices, they were content to follow us around as we made purchases at the Salvation Army store and several garage sales. To the new household, Pete's mom contributed cooking utensils and dishes (which I doubted would get much use), and I was able to supply sheets and towels and some accessories from our own extras. By Sunday, the place looked comfortable. However, when Pete brought in his stereo equipment, I wondered how long their arrangement would last before the Montoyas kicked them both out. There was enough potential volume to destroy the neighborhood.

Then we got to matters of transportation. Brad had planned to bicycle to work, but I put my foot down. His working hours were too erratic for that. We would furnish a vehicle, Paul's old truck, which was in very good condition, but he would have to pay for the insurance after this quarter. I hoped it wouldn't come to that. If Brad would just go back to school...

When Paul drove me back to the airport Sunday, I clung to him. "I hate to go," I said. "I wish I could be here. I wish I could make him go back to school. It's a long way to Houston and I miss you."

He smiled. "I miss you too. This moving out is a confidence builder for Brad. It's part of growing up." He saw my concern and added, "Don't worry, Rach. We've been through worse than this. He's a great kid, and..."

I squeezed his hand. "I know. I believe in him too." Then they called my plane.

* * *

I know I got to work somehow Monday, but I'm not sure how. I was preoccupied with Brad and his immature choices. Somehow, magically, Alicia jarred me out of autopilot. "Rachel!" She stood at my door, a soda in one hand and a cup of tea in the other. "I'm excited. Do you have time to talk to me now."

She handed me the tea, and I motioned her to a seat. "This must be about your trip. Tell me about it."

Getting the "Star Treatment"

"I'm going Wednesday morning bright and early. I'll be in Pembroke at eleven, and, Rachel, they're picking me up and driving me to Oakville. No busses or limos or anything. We'll go to lunch and then tour the building, and I'm meeting with a couple of people and Mr. Grant and his wife are taking us out to dinner. Me! I mean, I can't believe it." Alicia was tapping rapidly to the rhythm of her words. I must have looked at her hands because, suddenly conscious of what she was doing, she stopped in mid tap. "Oh, sorry. Tomás finds this very annoying. It's nervous energy."

I smiled. "It's a shame to waste all that enthusiasm on a desk. But that sounds exciting. I know you're going to get a lot out of this trip. It sounds like it's going to be fun too. Be sure to tell everyone hello for me."

"I will. I just wanted to let you know I'm going to make sure nothing will fall through the cracks while I'm gone. Judy and I are getting together at ten. She's going to cover for me, and if something comes up she can't handle, I'm going to have a pager with me, so I can call her right back. She's also going to round up a laptop with a modem for me to take. Won't that be great! I'll be able to transcribe notes at night and send messages to you and Judy. I'll be back in the office first thing Monday."

"Sounds like you're doing a thorough job planning for this. I like the idea of your having a laptop too because you're likely to wind up with some programming help at PWE. Might I offer a suggestion?"

"Sure."

"Alicia, one of the main reasons I was eager for you to go is to reduce your workload so you can do the things you enjoy. So please, don't step up the pace. If you need to spend additional time at PWE or go back, that's fine. Why don't you take Monday off? I think you're entitled to some comp time."

"I can't. That's putting too much pressure on Judy. You're right, Rachel. I need to slow down. I know I like to run at things—Tomás says sometimes I'm like a freight train. I'll take it easier. I promise. But I am excited. I'll see you before I go. I'll be here all day today and tomorrow."

"Good. Take off early tomorrow and rest a bit. I'm sure you'll need to pack and spend some extra time with your family."

"I will, Rachel." She looked at her watch. "I've got to go. There's so much to do. Thanks for everything." She stood up quickly and walked to the door.

"You're welcome," I said to her retreating back, "and thanks for the tea." All that energy wrapped up in one human being. Charlie had said Alicia was a gem and he was right. I thought back to a poet who wrote of someone "burning with a hard gem-like flame," and I worried that Alicia too might burn out. As I took a couple of sips of the tea, my thoughts drifted from Alicia to Brad. I wondered how he was doing in his new apartment and if he were still happy with the job. I hoped not.

"Off on one of those island trips, lady?"

I jumped, but quickly regained my composure. "Sorry, Tom. I'm afraid I was thinking about my son, the hamburger king. What's up?"

"I know you were interested in how the plans for the Grand Tour are coming along and thought I'd bring you up to date."

"Please do."

Winning Approval

Tom told me the informal meetings had gone well. The Marketers had decided to visit our "old" customers first with Katy covering San Antonio, Austin, and Houston. Tom and Justin would make Dallas-Ft.Worth, Tulsa, and Oklahoma City, and Stuart would go to New Orleans and Baton Rouge. Then for new business, Justin and Tom would travel to Mississippi (Tom's territory) and Alabama (Justin's territory); Katy would go to Florida and Stuart to Georgia. Tom anticipated the trips would take between four and six working days over two weeks. Preparation time was expected to take about a week with each of the marketers using that time to renew old contacts and make new ones.

"Was everyone satisfied with this plan?"

Tom grinned. "We dickered quite a bit. The only thing that was not up for negotiation was Georgia. Stuart insisted on going there." Tom laughed. "I think Stu has designs on PWE,"

I smiled. "So when is all this to take place?"

"Old customers, next week. New customers the week after. The only question is, things have been pretty quiet over there in Altis' corner. I've been delegated the task of checking on the feasibility of the project. Do you see any *problemos* with our proceeding?"

"I don't see any problem with visiting old customers, but before you all head into uncharted waters, let me check with Elroy Grant. TYH is in his division."

"So is there a reason you wouldn't check with Altis? He's still in charge, right?" (Oops! I almost slipped up. It wasn't my place to announce Altis' coming departure.) "Sure he is," I said, "but I know Elroy a lot better. He is the best one to advise me how to proceed. I'll get back to you as soon as I know for sure." While Altis' potential exit was not exactly a well-kept secret, it is the rule in most big companies to allow those announcements to be made within the normal framework—top down. (For those unfamiliar with corporate politics, my bit of subterfuge is not considered dishonest, but rather a part of "the code.") However, true to form, my explanation *appeared* to satisfy Tom, although I guessed he saw right through it.

When Tom left, I phoned Elroy. "I was going to call you," he told me. He had heard Alicia was coming Wednesday and wanted to let me know they would take good care of her. In fact, Maggie and he had invited Bill Rosen and Joanne Jackson to join them at Kirkland's for dinner Wednesday night. Bill and Joanne would handle Alicia's two days in Oakville, seeing that she learned what she needed to know. "They've offered to do the royal tour since I won't be in town Thursday and Friday," he told me, "but don't worry. She's in our care until we put her back on the plane." This information was delivered without pause. Just like Elroy. He had covered the pick up and the two days, and had put Alicia safely back on the plane without taking a breath. "Now for some other business," he continued. "The clock is ticking. I want to get up there in the next three weeks. Altis needs to be sent off by the middle of November.

This is getting perilously close to the holidays, and you know how I feel about that. Given what's going on there, when's the best time?"

Now Elroy Grant knew he didn't need my invitation—but I appreciated his asking." I suggested the week of October 31. "I want you to meet Katy, Tom, Justin and Stuart. They won't be here if you come any earlier," I explained. "They are going on the road to see customers next week, and, with your approval, they'll be soliciting new business in the South the following week. That's something I wanted to ask you about. In light of the current president's past position on new business, do you want me to sign off on week two of their trips, or should we wait until you've settled things here?"

"What do you think?"

"Morale is high and they are raring to go, so my vote is *yes*."

"Then let's do it. No reason to wait. I'm glad to see a little action in Houston. Our Management Council met last week and discussed what to do with To Your Health, sell it or make it profitable. Believe it or not, by unanimous vote we decided to go for black ink."

"I'm glad to hear it."

"How about your Marketing people? Is Stuart Kennedy shaping up or..."

"I'm not sure, Elroy. Let's see how these trips go. They were his idea."

"Okay, the jury is still out on him. How does the place look now that you've got it redecorated?"

I sighed. "More like home but no real substitute."

"Nothing is ever a real substitute," said Elroy. "I like the way you're handling things. I'm proud of you." Elroy was a true mentor, not in any way a parent. He knew when to be encouraging and when to overlook my plaintive bid for sympathy. The discussion was over—for now.

I headed for the coffee room. As I passed Judy's desk, she looked up. "Rachel, I think you should know that Justin needs to see you. He's come by twice and your door was closed. He waited around for a while then said he'd be back. Do you want me to call him and tell him you're available?"

"Thanks, Judy. I'll see if he wants to talk now," I said walking toward the coffee room. A cup of steaming tea in my hand, I headed toward Justin's office. He was just leaving. "Oh, I've come at a bad time," I said.

"No," he grinned. "I was just coming to see you. Have you got a few minutes?"

"I do," I responded, sitting in a chair facing the newly purchased picture of snowy mountains with a Swiss chalet to the right. "I love your picture. It makes me want to head for Steamboat Springs."

"Do you ski?" asked Justin.

"Not me. I'd love to look at the scenery with a warm cup of chocolate and a blazing fire. But that's not what you wanted to talk about."

Asking for a Salary Increase

"Maybe it is. Rachel, I need a raise," he blurted out. "I don't know if you are the one to handle it since you're here for a short time, but if not, I could use some advice on how to get one."

"Justin, help me out. I'm not really sure I understand. You're definitely in for the five percent we discussed based on your move into Marketing. I gather that's not what we're talking about."

"You know I've got a new baby. Everything is so expensive."

"I understand."

"Rachel, I'm not very good at this. I'm not sure how all this works, but I do know that Katy hasn't been here as long as I have, and she's making more than I am."

"Okay, now I understand." (You may be wondering why I didn't ask Justin how he learned about Katy's salary. I knew it could have only come from one of three sources: Katy, Tom, or

Stuart. I was sure then, as I am now, that it's a mistake for supervisors to venture into espionage or look for someone to blame when they hear these disclosures, so I chose not to follow up on this one.)

"I have a lot of respect for you," continued Justin, "and if I'm out of line, I hope you'll tell me, Rachel, but somehow it doesn't seem fair."

"Justin, I can't promise anything, but I will look into this and get back to you."

"Thanks Rachel, I couldn't ask for anything more."

"Maybe not, but would you mind terribly if I give you some advice?"

"No, I'd like to hear anything you can offer me."

"I really want to be sure. Unsolicited advice is generally worthless."

"I know. I've given some of that myself, and when I've gotten it, I've tended to tune it out, but in this case, it's invaluable, so please..."

"Okay. I offer this not as criticism but as something to consider for the future. Justin, there are three taboos in asking for money."

He shook his head. "I have a feeling I've cornered the market."

I smiled. "Well, listen and judge for yourself. *First, avoid saying you need money.* What you need or don't need is your concern—but it isn't thought to be To Your Health's. In business, salaries are economic transactions based on performance and contribution, not entitlements, so what you *need* isn't relevant to this discussion."

"Oh, that makes sense. I've never heard it put that way, Rachel. But what do you say instead?"

"You say, 'I'd like to discuss my salary.'"

"That does sound better and easier to say too. But there's more, so tell me."

"Okay, here's the second taboo. There's an unwritten rule in most organizations that pay is confidential. That means, people usually don't discuss their salaries with each other. I don't mean to imply it never happens, and if you know what others are being paid (and you trust the data you receive) it's good information, that is, if you understand the salary structure and those factors that are considered in determining pay. *However, when you're negotiating a raise with a manager, it does you little good to bring up someone else's salary.* That's a distraction from the most important thing, which is getting paid based on your own merit, not someone else's. With many managers, bringing up another's salary is a red flag and could easily turn into a discussion about how and why you obtained that information."

"I'm glad I made these mistakes with you, Rachel. I know you're not like that."

"Justin, you don't know that for sure, but this time your guess is right. You're relatively new at this game that is business, and I want you to succeed. That's why I'm sharing this with you. I hope you're not offended. I know I sound critical."

"I appreciate your advice. You said there was a third taboo?"

"Yes, there's one more. *You said it wasn't fair. In an economic transaction like pay, that's not exactly a winning argument.*"

"Come to think of it, I know that argument rarely works. My parents taught me that when I was a boy. I should have known better. Now I know what I shouldn't do, Rachel, would you mind telling me the right way?"

"Sure. Approach a salary discussion as you would any important business transaction. In the first place, you'll want to do a little market research. That includes how the company is doing as well as what others are receiving who are doing similar work."

"Doesn't that contradict what you just told me? I mean if I know what Katy is making...."

"If you learn what someone else is making, just file that away as another piece of information. The important thing is, don't use it as part of your argument. There are other good sources of salary information. Read the newspapers and learn what other companies are paying people who are doing your kind of work with your level of experience. You should also keep up with trade journals and other types of employment information. You might even check the pay for jobs advertised on the internet. Factor in any special qualities that impact your desirability. What have you contributed in the past? What about your education and experience? This sounds like a lot of trouble, but if you want to get a good result, it helps a lot. It's also important to know how your company is doing financially. Right now TYH is at a crossroads. However, the fact that PWE has acquired it is definitely a good sign.

"Next, and this is a critical factor, consider *what has changed* since your last raise. Is your job the same? Have you taken on more work? Is it more complex now? Have you added new skills? These are critical points for the discussion. Add to that your increased contribution and performance. Make sure your supervisor knows what you're contributing. This is an important ongoing responsibility if you want to be successful. There are a lot of people who believe if you get in there and work your heart out, you'll get the rewards you're looking for."

"Are you saying that hard work doesn't get it?"

"Not at all. But what I am saying is, hard work just isn't enough. The work you do must be recognized as significant, and your commitment to the job and the company, obvious."

"How can you be sure your work is significant? I mean if you're just at the early part of your career, people may not see that."

"You're right. That's why caring and dedication are so critical. Early on you must prove you're worthy of increased responsibility, and the only way you can do that is to go the extra mile, pay attention to detail, and not align yourself with people who complain about the company. That's important. You've got a good attitude, Justin. That will take you a long way."

"Not if I don't learn the taboos. Right?"

"I think people will line up to help you. You're an asset to any organization."

"Does that mean I stand a good chance of getting a larger raise?"

"What it means is, I promise to look into it and get back to you as soon as I can—either way."

"What do people do when they're not working with someone as willing to help as you are, Rachel?"

"Well, I've known of supervisors who try to distract you or change the subject by bringing up their own pay or other side issues. What I've learned is, let them have their say, but don't ever go down those conversational byroads with them. When they've finished, ask when they can get back to you about the raise."

"What if they just say *no*?"

"Ask what the problem is. You can't move forward until you're aware of the obstacles. Right? I mean there are many legitimate reasons besides your performance why that could be the answer."

"What if they just put you off?"

"Then set a date for follow up. That shows you're serious and gives them time to work on things."

"So, in keeping with your good advice, Rachel, when shall we plan to follow up?"

I laughed. "I think my advice is too good, Justin. Let's make it next Friday. If you're not here, then you can call me. Okay?"

He agreed and pulled out the latest baby pictures. I admired them and left.

NOTES TO MENTORING FILE

Explaining How the System Works

One of the principal roles of a mentor is to call upon her own experience to clarify to the individual how best to handle career or pay issues. This is one of those situations when giving advice is most helpful.

Example: Three Taboos when Asking for More Money

1. Asking for an increase is a business transaction. Rather than saying you need money, say you'd like to discuss your salary.

2. Bringing up what someone else is being paid may work against you. Organizations can always explain discrepancies. Discussing someone else's salary is a distraction and not material to your own request. In addition, most organizations frown on employees discussing salary issues with one another.

3. Bringing up issues of fairness rarely wins an argument.

What to Do

➢ Before the meeting, do market research to see (1) how the company is doing, and (2) what someone with your skills and in your position should be making.

➢ What has changed since the last increase? Is the job the same? Has the level of work or complexity increased? What about your increased contribution or performance? These are the compelling issues that most support your case.

➢ Be sure your supervisor is aware of your contributions on a continuing basis.

CHAPTER 11

Lead, Follow and Get Out of the Way

Make your friends your teachers and mingle the pleasures of conversation with the advantages of instruction.

— Baltasar Gracián, *The Art of Worldly Wisdom*

More of the letter:

A t first you seemed like a dynamo fixing the place up, worrying about the business, focusing on our petty squabbles, sharing your special brand of wisdom. Then, all of a sudden, you stepped back And said, 'it's all yours. I'm here if you need me.' What could you see that we couldn't? How were you able to pick the right moment? I'm still wondering about that.

I wish I were as brilliant as the letter implies. I smile thinking back to what I learned in Houston under the tutelage of one very wise man. I'll get back to that. It was Tuesday evening, and I was thinking about the day as I pulled out of my parking place. There had been an unusual flurry of activity right outside my office with Alicia getting ready to go to PWE and Judy preparing to step into her shoes for a couple of days. Most of the morning I kept the door closed and stayed out of the arena. When I left for a meeting, I noticed Alicia deep in conversation with Stuart. As I passed them, he stopped me. "Alicia tells me she's headed for Oakville. Sounds exciting."

"I think so," I said responding in the most jovial manner I could muster. Things had been pretty sticky since my last meeting with Stuart, and I welcomed any opportunity to pierce the thickening wall between us.

"You know, I might be in the vicinity myself soon," he added.

"So I've heard."

"Maybe you could arrange a meeting between me and Elroy. As long as I'm in Georgia anyway, I might as well visit PWE."

"When you know what day you'll be there, I'll give him a call and see if he's available. He is planning to come here the week of October 31st, and I know he'll want to meet *everyone*," I pointed out thinking that might change his mind. It didn't.

"Sure. I'll let you know when I can be in Oakville."

"I'll see what I can do," I said. I wondered whether Elroy would welcome his visit or if he'd even be there.

A note was waiting for me at home, pasted on the door with a Band-Aid. It was from Lucien. "You're invited for dinner and some stimulating, witty conversation (mostly provided by you). No RSVP necessary. Seven okay?
Lucien
P.S. Lizzy is making stuffed chicken breasts—a delight not to be missed."

I smiled. The turkey sandwich I had brought home for dinner would definitely keep.

Lucien was right. Beth's stuffed breasts were a culinary miracle. I tried to turn down the hot cinnamon apple cobbler but to no avail. Lucien gave me a taste of his and all was lost. With dinner over, we settled in the living room. "How are things at home?" he asked. "Brad still at the grill?"

I nodded. "He is for now—and settled in his own apartment. I keep wondering what happened."

Learning the Knowledge and Skills to Succeed

"He's just a boy trying to become a man," said Lucien handing me several sheets of paper. "That's why I think you'll be interested in this article I've been working on. I'd like to get your comments." I started to put them aside to read later, but it was obvious that he wanted me to read them right then. "It's about education with the emphasis on the 'small *e*,'" he said. "It's how we become equipped with the knowledge and skills to survive and succeed in today's complex world." The article was titled "Lost and Found." I was intrigued. In it Lucien wrote of the many changes that had happened in America: about working families in which both parents had left the influencing of their children to day care, to television and to a public school system under siege; about massive numbers of people from many lands moving into our country and not being assimilated into the traditions and ideas that form the cornerstone of our freedom and independence; about a "culture of compromise" in which happiness was substituted for aspiration in an effort to make everything fair.

He wrote of the breakdown of our system of Education (with a capital E) as the result, not the cause, of these situations. "With the decline of the two-parent family, the traditions, and the culture has come a public school system plagued with too many competing ideologies and too few standards."

I looked up. "What do you think of it so far?" he asked.

"Let her finish, Lucky," said Beth, refilling my cup with ginger tea. "Rachel needs a chance to think about what you're saying. It's complex stuff."

I smiled. "Thanks for giving me a minute to put my thoughts together," I said leaning forward in the overstuffed chair. "It's very thought-provoking, Lucien. I get the impression you think we're making a mistake when we blame the problem on our public school system."

"Right. You get what you ask for. We brought in the children who hadn't learned about family, culture, tradition, and aspirations, and we told the schools to teach them. Then we insisted that it be done in overcrowded classrooms and with absolutely no discipline. We hired teachers and told them, 'Get it done,' and then we tied their hands with one-size fits all curricula, insisted it be taught in several languages, and that no one fail." He said, punctuating each idea with a slap on his leg. "When the experiment failed, we blamed the schools. The truth is, it's our fault. We abandoned our responsibility. So now, we get to reap what we've sown."

"Your article is entitled 'Lost and Found.' I'm hoping you're going to suggest an answer. Right?"

"I wouldn't be so arrogant as to think I've found one, but something I think would help is if we could stop turning our heads and looking the other way." His voice softened. "Look, Rachel, you're the one who actually gave me the idea for this. Here you are at TYH for only a short time, but rather than be a typical do-nothing manager, you've taken on the responsibility to do something worthwhile to help others. That's what's needed, more people caring, more people passing down the stories of our cultures and traditions, in short, more mentoring."

"You won't find me disagreeing with that," I said, "but like it or not, we can't stop the world."

"No, we can't," he responded, "but neither can our society survive in a system that wails against traditional values, whines about 'fairness,' and teaches people they are entitled to its fruits without effort. And speaking of fruits, Lizzy, do you have another piece of that apple cobbler?"

"Life isn't fair, Lucky, and the answer is *no*. If you eat any more of it, I won't be responsible for what happens to your cholesterol. Here, have some more tea," said Beth, refilling his cup.

Passing down Values and Culture

"Today's world is a complex place full of ambiguities," he continued, "but history teaches us some important lessons about how civilized people pass down their values and culture to their young. Take your pick. I'm intrigued by stories I read about the Plains Indians. Did you know, Rachel, that from the beginning of his life a young Crow boy was taught everything he needed to succeed in their world? Everyone in the tribe contributed to his education. They made sure he learned his responsibilities to the tribe and the warrior traditions, that he knew what steps he must take to become a full fledged member, and he understood clearly what the standards were."

"Life was simpler then," I said, picturing a world where values were clear and understood by all.

"Socially perhaps, but in some ways it was more complicated. Throughout this learning period, the young man became part of the social structure, mentored by those who had proven themselves and receiving the counsel and advice of tribal elders. There were many skills to acquire: tracking, hunting, fighting, living off of the land to name just a few. At some point the youth had to prove his character and ability if he wished to be accepted into the war parties and to sit in the Councils. His older years were spent replenishing the tribe by mentoring the young.

"And that's not an isolated example. In some African tribes, a young man was taught all the hunting skills he needed and then, as a rite of passage, was sent by himself with only a spear for a weapon, to kill a lion. The elder, who had been his primary coach, followed some distance behind the young man, concealing himself in the underbrush. His purpose was to make sure the youth didn't get into trouble. Once the young man proved himself, he became a full-fledged member of the tribe.

"What these and other stories suggest to me, Rachel, is a natural progression of training and preparing people for the challenges they face. I think of it in very simple terms: lead, follow *and* then, get out of the way."

"That's an intriguing idea, Lucien," I interjected.

Process—Lead, Follow and Get Out of the Way

"Listen, and tell me if it doesn't make sense, Rachel. The *lead* part is the knowledge and skills passed down through the stories of the esteemed elders and learned by observing the warriors, who have earned the title of role model by proving themselves in the arena. They live the life to which the young person aspires. In short, they lead by example, not as distant icons but rather as mentors, accessible to their students and honored for their achievements."

"I like that image. I know full well, Lucien, that there are people out there who do that. I've been very fortunate to work with a few of them myself, including Elroy Grant, whose name I've mentioned to you."

"On more than one occasion."

I laughed. "So that's the *lead*. What about *follow*? Is that like the coach who trails behind the young African tribesman to make sure he doesn't get into trouble?"

"In a way, yes. *Following* is an important stage of the mentoring relationship. It's that link between doing something under the tutelage of someone who's been successful and actually doing it on your own."

"I know what you mean. I remember my algebra class. When the teacher was there, everything seemed so simple, but when I did the homework, I couldn't believe how hard it was."

"That's exactly my point. When you returned to class the next day, your algebra teacher was available to assist you with the problems you had trouble with—that is, if you had the initiative to ask for help. That's the interim step that can spell the difference between success and failure." He stood up and began pacing. "Rachel, I'm disturbed when I hear managers delight in bringing new people into their organizations and using a philosophy of *sink or swim*. I don't believe we can hold someone up indefinitely to keep him from 'drowning,' but neither should we continue to operate based on a philosophy that considers employees *disposable*. The cost is too high—to our society, to our country, and to the spirit that says we count all people as important. Sometimes we just have to look back at the forces I've already described and ask ourselves, how can we do better?"

"I see what you mean, Lucky, I mean Lucien." I said.

Beth smiled. "It's okay. You're family."

Lucien glowered. "Is it okay for Rachel to call you Lizzy?"

She frowned. "No, it's not. I don't like that name. It sounds like a reptile. I'm not sure it's okay for you to use it, Lucien."

I smiled. "Don't worry Beth, I won't use it. I value your friendship too much."

Lucien continued, "So you see, the concept of *following* is to understand that people need to experiment a bit and then have a friendly counselor to whom they can turn for guidance. The reason I think of that as *follow* is because at this stage, the adviser assumes a more passive role. It is now up to the learner to seek the advice or listening ear of the mentor."

"And if he doesn't know enough to ask?"

"There's an old saying. Experience is the best teacher. The only problem is the exam comes before the lesson."

"I'd hate to name the many things I've learned that way. But being a passive mentor is not easy for me," I said. "When you've got so much invested in someone's success, it's hard to stand back and watch her make mistakes."

"It is, but that's an essential part of learning," responded my teacher. "When a person decides to seek further guidance, advice, or feedback, she tends to be more receptive to the information than if it is offered by another. Also, because she asked for it, she probably feels more free to make her own decision on its value."

"It sounds like 'getting out of the way' may be the simplest part of all."

"Not necessarily, Rachel. Consider this: how does one know when the relationship between mentor and pupil is over?"

"I guess it's when one or the other decides, isn't it?"

"Some mentoring relationships end when the mentor sees in the person the maturity and judgment to make it on his own, or the individual recognizes her own need to fly solo. Some evolve into a collegial relationship. Occasionally, there is a battle of wills followed by an abrupt ending. There are issues of control and approval in almost every mentoring relationship. The mentor has to realize his advice may not always be taken, and the individual at some point must free himself from the need for the mentor's approval. For some people that requires a complete break. Sometimes the relationship breaks off too soon, leaving both individuals not completely satisfied. Then, there are some people who think they can fly solo before they are ready."

"Some people aren't very strong in judgment. I know my sense is that might be a problem for both Stuart and Katy."

"Maybe so, but don't be too sure," he responded. "Katy's judgment is obviously maturing. The first situation you described, the one with Super Health, required that you take the lead. You gave her some advice and followed up. Right?"

"Right. I thought she was going to backslide when Stuart entered the picture, but fortunately she got back on track and made the apology."

"The key is you taught her what to do. Then came the situation with the meeting. From what you told me, I surmised Katy realized she had messed up, and that's why she came to you. You didn't send for her. So, in this situation, your role was *following*."

"Ah, I get it. Stuart's situation is much more difficult. We seem to have a communication barrier that I can't get through," I said shaking my head.

"I suspect he's pretty disappointed and sees you as fair game."

"Yes, a goose. The problem is it's turned me off so much that every conversation we have seems to evolve quickly into a power struggle, and that's out of character for me. Frankly, I'm beginning to doubt that I'm the right mentor for him."

"You're probably right, Rachel, but at the same time, what he may need from you is what I call a *mentoring moment*."

"That's a concept new to me. What is it?" I asked.

"It just means that sometimes an individual can offer one of those flashes of insight or be part of a revelation that makes a difference in our lives even if a single piece of information is all this person can provide," responded Lucien.

"I can relate to that. Once I was in a new assignment and working with someone who was very rigid and authoritarian. I was having a tough time and didn't know what to do, but a manager at PWE saw what was happening, took me aside and gave me some important advice that helped. But how do you identify when that moment comes?"

"You'll know. Someone once said, 'When the student is ready, the teacher appears.'"

"I just feel so helpless when it comes to Stuart."

"You're anything but helpless. The moment simply hasn't come yet, but I think it will. Just don't get invested in that insight coming from you. It could be Elroy Grant or Charlie Rothstein who tells Stuart what he needs to know."

"I hope someone does," I sighed. "He's a lot more lost than he realizes. So 'getting out of the way' is a decision based on judgment. I like that, but I'm not sure how you tell if the person has enough judgment to go it alone."

"Let me make a comparison to the relationship of a parent with a young adult. The teenage years represent the youngster's struggle for independence and the parent's for control. The young adult thinks he can make it on his own. Yet, when he needs something, he often doesn't even consider using his own resources. Mom and Dad are available, and they can help."

"Tell me about it. I've got the perfect example at home. Brad decided he was grown up enough to have his own apartment. Next thing we knew he had his hand out. "

"Right, and from what you say, you didn't trust his judgment enough to fill it up with money. Instead, you and Paul took him shopping. But at some point, every young adult has to demonstrate to his parents that he can make it on his own."

"Well his stint as king of hamburgers sure hasn't proven anything to me."

"Of course it hasn't, but you haven't made the mistake some parents do who unwittingly hurry the process along by confusing physical size with emotional maturity and then find themselves with a boomerang kid. A young girl marries too soon, divorces, comes home with a baby. A young man leaves home and when things go wrong, returns to his old room and his old ways. This is the analogy I'm making. The role of the mentor, like the role of the parent, is to help someone build judgment and independence. So how do you know you're there? By the hard choices that people make. By their ability to overcome obstacles. By their accepting the consequences of their actions. And when you see that in the person you are mentoring, it's time to 'get out of the way.'"

"What if you never see it?"

"Perhaps you've taken over the controls. Birds fly when their parents push them out of the nest, and not until."

"What sort of relationship, if any, can you have after that?"

"It depends. With some people, you give up contact. The end of the relationship is just that. With others you back off and see what happens. I've had some people I mentored become friends, but I must tell you, that happens less often than the other two situations."

There was a lull in the conversation, and Beth took that opportunity to ask about Paul and how we had met. From this we turned to the accidents of time and place from which one creates friendships that last a lifetime. It was luck, sheer luck, that had placed me across the hall from the Powells. Sometimes fortune smiles.

NOTES TO MENTORING FILE

Process Summary

In the first phase of the process, the mentor takes the *lead*. In this stage, the mentor plays a very active role, teaching, coaching, and explaining. The person being mentored seeks to profit from the knowledge and skills, which are exemplified by the mentor's achievements.

The *follow* phase is a gradual transition as the lead moves from mentor to mentee. In this stage, the mentor becomes a consultant, advisor, counselor and sounding board to the person mentored. The key to success is to continue the process at some level even if the mentee doesn't seek counsel. The solution might be some form of "how's it going" process or *check-in* on a regular basis so the mentor can continue to provide limited feedback or information and so the mentee doesn't feel cut off .

Getting out of the way represents a challenge for both mentor and mentee. There are issues of control and approval in almost every mentoring association, and quite often one party feels more strongly than the other that it is time for the relationship to end. Important considerations for *getting out of the way* include: the mentee's independence and judgment and the mentor's sense of how much more she can offer. Sometimes the relationship becomes collegial, but often it breaks off completely as the mentee "leaves home."

Mentoring Moments

These are powerful revelations or pieces of information that make a difference in our lives sometimes offered by an individual who is not our mentor.

CHAPTER 12

Problems and Problem Solving

A word is dead/When it is said,/Some say.
I say/It just begins to live,/That day.

— Emily Dickinson, *Poem*

It was Thursday and I was looking forward to a quiet day at work. I had an early appointment with Lily Sheldon to discuss Justin's salary, a couple of meetings to attend, and phone calls to return. Maybe I could leave early and spend the weekend in Oakville. My discussion with Lucien had been an eye opener, but I wasn't sure how we could apply it to Brad's situation. He certainly wasn't living up to the "warrior" tradition—at least not in my eyes, but Lucien had pointed out the transition he was attempting to make toward manhood. That was something to think about.

I had gotten just that far in my inner wanderings when I noticed my gas gauge perilously close to "E." I stopped at a gas station to fill up and discovered a tire was low and that the "service" station I was in didn't change tires. They didn't do windows either. I finally found a "full service" station; however, there were several cars ahead of mine, and that meant I would probably not make my appointment with Lily Sheldon to discuss Justin's salary. When I tried to call the office, I got a busy signal, so I was unable to tell Judy about my situation. I finally reached Lily, and we rescheduled for eleven. By the time I got to work, I was feeling frazzled, so much so that I was oblivious to the fact that Judy wasn't wearing her usual smile. Her voice, however, was not so easy to ignore. She was rattled.

"Rachel, can I talk to you a moment?" she asked.

"Sure, come in. What's going on?"

She sat down. "I don't want to be petty," she said. "It's not like me."

I agreed.

Overworking Others

"My phone has been ringing off the hook. Alicia has called me so many times I've lost count."

"Is she having a problem?"

"No, but she's creating one. She's called to check on things that I have on my list, to ask me to make some calls for her, and to follow up on messages. It's clear to me she thinks I don't have anything else to do, and what's more, that I'm incompetent. Let me show you the list she left me when she went to PWE. There is so much detail a second grader could do it in her sleep."

There was.

"This constant checking up is making me crazy. I know that she's 'over me,'" continued Judy, shaking her head, "so I can't tell her not to call. I'm not sure what I should say or do. I certainly can't get any of my normal work done. But about ten minutes ago was the last straw. She asked me to call Super Health to check on the order they gave Katy. I don't mind doing that, but it took me three phone calls to get her what she wanted. Each time she called she asked me to find out something else from Frank Manchester. Then she called back to see what he said and had another question. I felt foolish the third time I called him, and he sounded irritated. What worries me is that she's likely to call back with another question after this one."

"You've had quite a morning already, Judy. I can certainly testify to the number of calls, since I've had my share of busy signals trying to call in this morning. Alicia is a bundle of energy, and this is the first time she's been away from the office like this. I'm sure she trusts you. I certainly do. I don't want you feeling incompetent, but I'd like to talk with her the next time she calls. See how things are going and all."

Judy smiled. "Thanks Rachel. Oops, I hear my phone. I'll bet it's her."

It was Alicia, and she was excited. She told me about the dinner with Elroy, how friendly every one had been and how much she was learning. I listened, asked questions, and congratulated her on all she was doing. Then she asked to talk with Judy. "I don't think this is a good time to do that," I told her. "Judy's had a rough morning."

"Really?" asked Alicia. "I've talked to her a number of times, and she's seemed fine to me."

"I think that's the problem, I mean the number of calls. I know that you are making sure nothing slips, and I appreciate that. At the same time, the constant interruptions and the 'first-shoe' conversations are making a nervous wreck out of a very competent woman."

"Excuse me. I don't think I heard you right. Did you say 'first-shoe'?"

"I did. That's my name for those three-party conversations in which person one tells person two to ask person three a question. That's the first shoe falling. Then person one gets the reply and asks another question and the cycle goes back to the beginning. It's as if the first shoe is dropped, picked up, and dropped again and again. Person two keeps waiting for the second shoe to fall because that means the situation is concluded, but it can go on for a long time. So, person one gets her needs met, at the same time frustrating person two and annoying person three. Make sense?"

"I guess I've been person one today."

"Big time. My suggestion is (1) if it's something that is *extremely* important to handle right now, Judy will handle it, but you should provide all the information she needs to do that with one call. If she needs to check with someone, there are plenty of people available to ask. (2) If it's something that will require more questions depending on the answer, make the call yourself. (3) If it can wait, let it. You'll be back Monday and can take care of it then."

"I'm really sorry, Rachel. I didn't know that I was upsetting Judy."

"Judy is fine, just feeling a bit undervalued and overworked. I know I've said it before, but I do appreciate how conscientious you are, so I hope you understand what I've been saying."

"I do, Rachel. Can I ask Judy just one more question?"

"You can, if it's critical, but Alicia, she is over-committed right now, so please don't ask her to do anything else. If it's something simple, tell me and I'll do it."

"I thought I left a paper in my right hand desk drawer, and I need it faxed."

I got the information from Alicia, promising to look into it myself. Three minutes later she was on the phone. She found the paper in her briefcase, and I had her promise not to call again unless there was a hurricane or a flood.

A De-motivating Salary System

There went my quiet morning. Maybe the afternoon would be better? Wrong. It started out well enough. My discussion with Lily Sheldon about Justin's salary was enlightening. Talk about tinkering! The changes in the salary system the last two years of Altis Dunlop's regime as President of To Your Health had certainly been de-motivating for the Marketers. They were now on a salary plus semi-annual bonus based on sales. The problem was that the salary was paid at ninety percent as I had learned from Tom. So, for example, if your salary was forty thousand dollars, your pay was thirty-six thousand. I found it no coincidence that this new salary situation occurred at about the same time Tom Gaines stopped bringing in new customers. As for Justin, without a marketing manager present, no one had set his target. No wonder Justin was perplexed. He had received a nice raise (if you add in the ten percent) but the difference in his paycheck at ninety percent was very small. I also checked the situation with Katy's salary. It *was* slightly higher than his based on her education and a signing bonus. TYH was proud to have a Stanford graduate with Katy's grade point average and references.

I went back to my office to consider my dilemma. First, I decided to communicate with Elroy. I had a feeling he would want to look into the salary situation. I also needed to know when a *bona-fide* manager would be coming in so I could tell Justin something more than, "We'll get back to you." Elroy returned my call at three with instructions. I should look at Katy's target and assign the same one to Justin. When he came to Houston, he would be talking to Human Resources about the Marketing salaries. He didn't like the sound of what was going on, and he thought once the new regime was in place, the salary schedule would bear more resemblance to that at PWE. Until then, I was to "hold the fort." And then he chuckled.

I didn't. Somehow, nothing seemed particularly funny that day. "We'll get back to you"was the message for Justin, and "hold the fort" was mine. Thanks Elroy. I took a couple of deep breaths and started toward Justin's office. He wasn't there. Heading back for mine, I nearly ran into him. He was walking out of Tom's office and looked uncharacteristically grim. He brightened momentarily when he saw me, and at my suggestion, we went back to his office to talk. We talked about the target, the ninety percent and I promised him more and better answers soon. I smiled; he didn't. "Justin," I said, "I know things are a bit unsettled but...."

Being Treated with Respect

"It's not that, Rachel. It's Tom. I know I sound like I'm complaining, but I thought he wanted to help me."

"I thought so too. What's happened?"

"I've been to his office twice today trying to set something up, and he's let me know he's too busy to talk."

"That must be frustrating."

"It has been. I don't know how long he's going to put me off or when I can expect to get some help from him."

"What has he said about that?"

"I'll get back to you—kid."

"Kid?"

"Yes, Rachel, and I don't like that. But I'm trying to get some promised help, and I don't know how much I can expect if I let him know he is getting to me."

"I don't think Tom means anything by it, Justin. Have you mentioned it to him?"

"Not in so many words."

"But you need to be explicit. Just let him know in a nice way that you expect to be called by your name. Say it in your own words, but make it clear. *I learned long ago that if you have to choose between being loved and being respected, go for respect. Love is freely given but respect is earned.*"

"You don't think he'll be insulted?"

"Not if you *focus on your reaction to his words rather than on him*. The only way you can stop it is by calling attention to it. Say something like, 'Tom, when you call me kid it makes me think you don't have any respect for me. I like you and I want us to have a good relationship.' You know what to say."

"I'll do it. But what about the fact that he doesn't seem to have any free time? Rachel, I know you must regard me as the biggest complainer around. It's just that..." His voice trailed off.

I waited for a moment before responding. "I don't think so. You're a high achiever, and you are going to shine, I promise. Since Tom doesn't seem to have time when you walk into his office, invite him to lunch, or catch him on a break. Then tell him you need five minutes, or ask him if you can make an appointment. What you want to do is set up a time when you can get together and have a real conversation. Walking into his office is like arriving at someone's house uninvited. See what I mean? Now if you need my help in any way, you've got it, but it's better for you if you do it on your own."

Justin promised to deal with his problem with Tom, and I hoped that Tom wouldn't make things any more difficult. "Stay out of it, Rachel," I kept telling myself. "Justin's got a spear and he can handle this lion." So I got a cup of tea and walked back toward the quiet of my office.

Interpersonal Style

Katy was sitting in the reception area with Judy, and she looked out of sorts. She followed me into my office. "What's up?" I said as cheerfully as I could. In the next few minutes I learned (1) she wanted more product training, (2) she was feeling left out because Justin was getting help from Tom, and (3) she wanted me to do something about it. Katy was clear, Katy was right, but Katy was not very diplomatic in delivering the message. Even so, I decided that now was not the appropriate time to point that out. She suggested I call Charlie Rothstein,

Manager of the Sugar Land plant. It was a good idea, and I wasted no time in complying.

"It must be telepathy," said Charlie. "I was just getting ready to call you. We've got our new mini-gelcaps coming out next month, and your marketers need to come over and learn all about them."

"Charlie, they are going on the road next week."

"Good. Then tell them to drop everything and get over here tomorrow at one. We'll put a little dog and pony show together for them so they'll have something great to hawk."

"What are these gelcaps for?" I asked.

"Mini-gelcaps, Rachel, that's the point. Most people hate to take vitamins because they taste bad, smell awful and are large enough for a horse. These are small and jam-packed with nutrition, and they smell sweet. Also, you don't have to eat a big meal to take them because they are coated. Ah, but I don't want to give away my whole pitch. They are also color-coded. Pretty cool, huh?"

"Sounds great. I'll get the message out. Hopefully everyone can attend. Charlie, what about some kind of full-blown product review for Katy and possibly Justin? Both are pretty new to the field and I know it would help them immeasurably."

"I'm not sure Justin needs product help. He's worked the retail end of the business, but let's give them both the opportunity. If they can stay later, I'll get someone to show them around. Okay?"

"That's fine. And Charlie, thanks."

I relayed the information to Katy, who nodded her approval. "You've said you don't want to go with Tom and Justin on some sales calls," I added. "Have you thought about asking Tom to go with you perhaps to meet some new customers in Houston?"

"I have, and I decided not to. Rachel, he's overloaded with his own and Justin's work. What would you think if I asked Stuart instead?"

What would I think? I shuddered at the thought. Stuart already had too much influence on Katy. "You decide," I told her. "If I can help you in any way, please let me know." When she left I had the mad urge to crawl under my desk. Today had started out to be so pleasant, but it had wound up to be a "crabby day" with a myriad of complaints and dissatisfactions. So far, I had resisted the mood. Judy was doing better, having recovered from hurricane Alicia, and she agreed to broadcast Charlie Rothstein's invitation to the "troops."

Immaturity

As I drove home, I decided to have a quiet evening. I would eat the turkey sandwich waiting in the refrigerator, brew some chamomile tea and curl up in bed with a good mystery. The phone was ringing when I walked in the door. "Rachel," said Paul, "I thought I'd bring you up to date on the latest." It seems that Brad had made plans to go to a football game the previous night with Pete Redfield, his roommate. His boss, however, called Brad about thirty minutes before they were to leave and asked him to work. Brad had claimed a sore throat.

"Oh, Paul," I moaned, "I thought we taught him better."
"Well, that's not the worst of it," he said. "The boss was at the football game and noted Brad's miraculous recovery."

"I take it our management-trainee is unemployed."

"He is. When he arrived at work today, he was told he was no longer needed."

"It's a hard lesson to learn, but he shouldn't have told a lie."

"I agree, but that's not all of it. He was so upset on the way home, he hit another car. But don't worry. He wasn't hurt."

"His fault?"

"He's the one who got the ticket. He's going to handle the fine."

"So how much is this going to cost us right now?"

"About four hundred, give or take. Our son had better start rethinking his life fast—before I discover child abuse."

"I know what you mean. Any hope he might come home?"

There wasn't. Now I was feeling crabby too.

* * *

I expected Friday to be uneventful. Katy, Stuart, Tom and Justin were making last minute arrangements for their trips. All four would be off to Sugar Land in the afternoon. Alicia was due to spend half the day at Perry Winkle Enterprises and would be back Monday. Frankly, I didn't miss any of them after Thursday. My suitcases were in the car, and Oakville, Georgia, was "on my mind." First thing that morning I checked the plane schedules and decided to catch the two o'clock plane to Pembroke. Paul was delighted when I called and said he would make reservations at our favorite Italian restaurant. When I asked about Brad, he said we'd talk about that later.

Solutions

Walking into the coffee room, I saw Justin and Katy in conversation. "Can I talk to you a minute?" asked Katy.

"Of course," I said.

"In your office? I'll be there in ten minutes. I just have to return one phone call."

"See you then," I responded, hoping we were not in the midst of another crisis. I glanced over in Justin's direction. He shrugged. I assumed our young warrior had put down his spear and the lion was roaring—at least, for now. At any rate, no hiding in the underbrush for me. Just as soon as I finished talking with Katy, I'd go straight to Tom's "den" and see what the problem was. "Rachel," I said to myself, "this is not what Lucien meant when he said 'mentors follow.'" No matter, I rationalized. The agreement Tom made to help Justin was with me, so I decided I had every right to check on how things were going.

"Rachel," said Katy, waking me from my reverie. "Did I startle you?"

"A little," I acknowledged. "I was deep in thought."

"Well, I'm here to apologize for yesterday," she said. "I was in a bad mood, and I shouldn't have snapped at you."

"Apology accepted," I responded, smiling. "And you did it so well too."

"I had a good teacher—and more than enough opportunities to practice. I'm hoping I can get to the point in my life when I don't have to do it regularly," said Katy. "I could tell by the way you looked yesterday that I came on much too strongly, although you were nice and didn't say a word about it."

"You know, Katy, you're a bit like a three-way light bulb that continuously glows at one hundred eighty watts. You're bright but sometimes too intense. That puts people off. Now if you could lower the wattage sometimes, others would come to realize what a warm, caring person you really are."

"I like that example about the light bulb, Rachel. I'll remember it."

"And I like you. You're fun to be around. Thanks for taking the time to come by and apologize. Most people would have just waited for it to blow over."

"I didn't want to leave for two weeks on the road without telling you I was sorry. You've really been so much help to me." With that, she turned and left. Lucien was right. Katy's judgment was improving. So were her interpersonal skills. I looked at my watch and decided I had just time enough to talk with Tom before he went with the others to Sugar Land. He was in his office talking on the phone, his feet on the desk. When he saw me he smiled broadly and waved, an expansive gesture that summoned me into the throne room. A subsequent signal indicated he would be off the phone in one to two minutes, so I decided to wait. "To what do I owe the pleasure of your company?" he began as he returned the phone from his shoulder to its cradle.

"Tom, I need your help," I said, staring at the soles of his shoes and noting the rundown heel on the left one.

"You got it," he responded, leaning back in his chair and clasping his hands behind his head.

"Don't be so quick to decide."

"What's on your mind?" His feet returned to the floor. Then, a pause. "If it's about Justin, I told him to relax, take it slow. Everything's under control."

"It's just that—I think he and Katy need help. Tom, they're lost. They..."

"Hold it, Rachel," he said sitting up straight in his chair. "I like you. You're doing good things, but I need to take care of business, my business. I can't adopt everyone, now can I?"

"Nor should you."

"Then?"

"I think I caught you at a bad time, Tom. I can come back later," I said, starting for the door, "but do me a favor and think about it. No one knows the selling business the way you do. You're our superstar. I'd hoped you would be willing to pass your knowledge on to Katy and Justin." He said nothing, so I stood at the door. "I can't believe you were always this good. Someone must have helped you along the way," I said, as I opened it.

"Come back for a minute, Rachel. No need to leave in a huff." His feet were back on the desk, and he seemed more relaxed. I sat down. For a moment he closed his eyes. "You're good. You ought to be in this business."

"I used to be," I responded.

"Okay, I'll admit I had some pretty good teachers. I learned the most from Sid Bell and a few others who took me around with them and showed me how it is done. That's for sure. I had to carry the water, and I was the butt of more than one joke. You know how salesmen are. Sid was the best."

"And you're the recipient of his legacy, Tom."

"Look, you've made your point. I want to help Justin, but he needs to be patient. I've got to get in touch with my contacts. First things first. Then I'll make more time for him, Rachel. He's a good kid."

"He's a fine young man," I countered, "and I know he'll appreciate your help—but Tom, he has contacts to call too, and it would help if..."

"Okay, you win," he sighed, "not because you're persistent, though heaven knows you are, but because, this time you're right. As I said before, you ought to go back into marketing. No one could resist your powers of persuasion."

"I think that's a compliment, isn't it? Anyway, while I've got you cornered, what about Katy?"

"I don't think so, Rachel. I've got one extra mouth to feed already. Stu said he was going to help Katy," he responded. "They get along well together."

So that's the way we left it. By two I was aboard a plane headed for Georgia.

Paul brought Brad along when he came to pick me up, and the three of us went to Luciano's in Pembroke for dinner. We had barely finished our salads when Brad brought up the accident. "I guess you heard about the truck, Mom." I had, and I was glad he wasn't hurt. He told me it was just a "fender bender." He was once again employed, he told me, but this was only a "stop-gap" job.

"What is it?" I asked.

"Delivering pizzas, but don't get excited, Mom," he continued, responding to my dazed look, "I'm not planning on staying there for long. It's just 'til my other job comes through."

"Other job?"

"Yes. I've been talking to the manager of the Rainbow Inn, and I think I might get a job there. They have to check my references first."

"Brad, are you sure you want to stay in this 'food business.' I mean what do you feel you got out of your job as management trainee?"

"Not much, I guess. It's hard working like that. You don't make any decisions. They called me a *management trainee*, but what they really meant was *grunt*. I was cleaning bathrooms and washing off tables. I understood the word *trainee*, but I don't have a clue what they meant by *management*."

I stifled the urge to agree. "That's not your future anyway, but telling them you had a sore throat!"

"I probably shouldn't have done that, Mom, but they didn't treat me fairly. They promised me something and didn't deliver. And they should have warned me rather than fire me."

I sighed. "I know it must seem that way. Still, I'm not sure there's any organization I know of that wouldn't have fired you for what you did. I hope you've learned something about the business world from that. What about the job you're in now?"

He pushed a lock of sandy hair back from his face and thought for a moment. "Not too great," he answered. "They told me to expect big tips, but some people are cheap. They tell you to keep the change and there's a quarter or less. If the pizza has one ingredient different from what they ordered, they complain to me. I didn't make it, and I don't like listening to their complaints. The only good thing is the freedom of driving around, but I'm not staying there. There's no future in it. I like the Rainbow Inn. It's a great restaurant, and I'm sure the tips will be much better."

"Where's the future in that? And what about school?" Paul rolled his eyes, an indication I would get nowhere by nagging. I looked away. Parenting can be difficult when you want so much for your child.

Brad went on, "Don't worry, Mom, I'm learning a lot about the business world." I doubted that. "I couldn't stay in this job, even if I wanted to. It doesn't pay enough. I never realized how much living on your own costs. And now Pete's parents want him to move out of our apartment and back home because of his grades." I felt a ray of hope. Brad could not possibly afford his apartment alone.

"So when is he moving?" I asked.

"He's not. Pete's got to the end of the semester to bring his grades up, and I'm sure he'll do it."

"Even with his paying half, I can't imagine that the pizza job is enough for you to make it on." He nodded in agreement. "That's where a good education comes in," I added.

"Uh huh," he responded, looking at his watch. I looked at Paul. He shrugged. I had said enough.

That was the only conversation I remember having with Brad that weekend. When we got back to the house, he made his apologies. My son, management trainee, pizza deliverer and soon-to-be-waiter had other commitments. My guess is he wanted to return to the serenity of his own place where no well-intentioned mother could nag him about his future. As I said earlier, you can't mentor your children. The emotional component is there, unspoken but ever-present.

CHAPTER 13

Stressful Situations

> *When we act on our own choices, we define our own future. The good news is we have the sense of being in control of our lives. The bad news is that it's our fault and there's no one else to blame.*
>
> — Peter Block, *The Empowered Manager*

Monday mornings are usually hectic. All the work left over from the rush to escape on Friday sits waiting for you, silent and menacing. It's always worse when you've made an early exit as I had. So I was pleasantly surprised when I entered my office to see my desk bare, no pink slips, nobody waiting. The Marketers were off on phase one of their sales trips, and I suspected there would be no news until their return. Judy looked up from her desk, smiled and returned to the papers she was typing. I noticed a small crystal vase with three silver roses in it. "Those are beautiful. Something special?" I asked.

"They're a peace offering from Alicia," said Judy. "Smart lady."

"You deserved it after last week. Did she say anything when she came in? Does she want me to call her?" The answer to both questions was *no*. "I guess I'll drop by and see how things went at Perry Winkle," I said.

"I wouldn't," responded Judy. "She's squirreled away in her office with the door shut, and she told me not to disturb her."

I could understand that. Alicia had been gone for several days, and she probably had some catching up to do. Just then Judy's phone rang. "Alicia's ready for me," said Judy with a grin. "I guess she wants to catch up on what happened Friday afternoon."

"Tell her I'd like to chat with her," I said.

Judy returned. Alicia was busy, she told me. She doesn't want to be interrupted, but when she had time, she'd come by and talk. So, I went back to my office and wrote a note to Elroy.

```
To: egrant@pwe.net
From: rachel@pwe.net

    Things are pretty quiet here. I'm in a
    waiting mode. Waiting to see the results
    of Alicia's visit to PWE, waiting to hear
    how the Marketers do on visiting old cus-
    tomers, waiting to see what you think
    when you visit Houston. How are things at
    PWE?

Rachel

P.S. Next week Stuart Kennedy is planning
to make some sales pitches in Georgia. I
think he'd like to visit PWE and meet you.
What do you think?
```

Thirty minutes later:

```
To: rachel@pwe.net
From: egrant@pwe.net
```

> Things are fine here, just the way you left
> them. I'll be away for the next two weeks,
> first at a conference and then in
> Scottsdale playing golf. In the meantime,
> tell Kennedy if you can wait, he can too.
> I'll meet him when I meet the others in a
> couple of weeks. I guess everyone has to
> wait some time. If you need me, you can
> catch me on my pager.
>
> Elroy

The morning dragged on. Around eleven I decided to see if Alicia was going to lunch. I stopped by her office. She was at her desk as usual, surrounded by papers. On her credenza was the laptop computer. She was busily pecking away at it and hardly looked up when I came in.

"How about lunch?" I asked.

She looked up briefly. "Judy is bringing me a sandwich. I'm just going to eat at my desk. There's so much going on, Rachel, you wouldn't believe it. I have to catch up or I'll go crazy." All of this she uttered without taking a breath.

"I'd like to know how things went," I ventured.

"I know. I know," she said, swinging around and facing me, "and I'll get back to you. Honestly, I will."

"How about getting together tomorrow?"

The tapping started, first slowly then gaining in momentum. It was clear I was making Alicia nervous. "I'll try. Okay?" The phone rang and she turned away. I was dismissed.

On the way back to my office I ran into Ron Corbin, the Assistant Controller who had been so helpful in finding money for my project. He smiled when he saw me. "Just the person I was looking for. Come with me, Rachel. I want to show you something. Then I'm going to buy your lunch in the most exclusive restaurant in town."

"I take it you mean the downstairs cafeteria."

"The same," he said guiding me toward his office. "Well, what do you think?"

"I think you've made my day," I said, admiring walls adorned with brightly colored geometric prints.

"That isn't all," he said. "Let's take a walk." So we went from office to office in the Accounting Department as I saw more walls decorated with flowers in splashy watercolors, impressionist posters, and formal oil paintings of bluebonnet fields.

"I love it, Ron. It lifts my spirits. How have people reacted?"

"More energy and better morale. It's amazing. My next step is to see if we can pipe in some music. What do you think?"

"I think it's a grand idea, Ron. What has the reaction been in Human Resources?"

"You mean Lily? She was a bit flustered at first, but I offered to send back any paintings she had a problem with, and she refused. Now, she's acting as if the whole thing were her idea. I saw a note she sent to Distribution, Computing Services, and Building Maintenance, suggesting they add some art work to their walls as well. Told them it would increase morale." He giggled. "The note came too late for Distribution. Their pictures were already on order and will be hung tomorrow. Want to see the memo? I made a copy of it. Come back to my office, and I'll show it to you."

Sure enough, Lily had taken the old adage, "If you can't beat 'em, join 'em" to heart. Now she wholeheartedly supported putting holes in those sterile walls. In fact, she actually gave out the number of the Frame Shop as a *recommended* place to buy. I wondered if she realized that Altis Dunlop, TYH president, would soon be history so she had abandoned some of his more rigid policies. Who knows? At any rate, I was excited by the results and grateful for the bright diversion to an otherwise bleak day.

Warning Signs

Tuesday came and went without any messages from Alicia, and I began to see a dangerous pattern forming. When I got ready to leave the office at 5:30, I noticed her door still closed. I knocked. "Alicia, are you in there?"

"Come in, Rachel," she said. "I was finishing up a couple of things before I go home." The stack of papers in front of her belied her assessment.

"Is everything all right?" I wondered.

"No problem. I want to make sure I've double checked a few things—then I'll be leaving; don't worry. I've got to make dinner, so the sooner I finish, the sooner I'll get out of here. See you later, Rachel," she said, turning back to her work.

So in spite of my pleas, she stayed. I felt a sense of responsibility for what was happening here. I had been the one who insisted that a visit to Perry Winkle Enterprises was the solution to her long hours. It appeared that the reverse was true. It had only made the rock heavier.

By the next morning, I resolved that if Alicia didn't come out for lunch, I was going in to get her. This had to stop. Her stress level must be at its peak. I know mine was. About ten thirty, Judy came to the door. "I'm worried about Alicia," she said. "I saw her in the rest room. Her eyes were all red. She looked like she had been crying."

I was out of my seat before Judy could finish and headed for Alicia's stronghold.

"Come in," she said to my persistent knock. Alicia sat in the midst of the paper, the laptop computer open on her desk. The picture of her family had been moved from its customary place on the credenza to a spot adjacent to the computer. She looked up at me, her eyes welling over with tears. "It's Roberto," she sniffed. It seemed that Alicia's eleven-year-old had received a failing grade in mathematics. Tomás and Alicia had had words about it last evening when she had gotten home at seven thirty.

She was too wrapped up in her work, he had told her. Perhaps she wanted to move into the office. If she couldn't handle her job and her children, then she would have to quit. He wasn't going to have his boys raised without a mother. That was that. "I've been crying all morning," she sobbed. "I don't know what to do, Rachel. My children and Tomás are my life, but I love my job too. You're so good at solving problems. What should I do?"

Whenever I find someone in the midst of an emotional situation, even though there might be logical answers, *I've learned to deal first with the emotions.* "You're having a rough time, Alicia. Is there anything I can do?"

"No, there's nothing. I just don't know how to please him and get all my work done. I don't want to quit, but I don't want to sacrifice my family either."

"You've been putting in long hours," I offered. "The trip didn't help I fear."

"Oh, but it did help. There were so many good ideas, I just need time to get them going."

"And you will, but right now you're feeling stressed. I want you to go home and rest for a couple of days. Be with your family. When you feel like coming back, we'll work together to find the right answer."

She rose. "I don't want to lose my family," she said.

"And you won't. Now, go."

"But my work!"

"Judy and I will figure things out. For now, you need to be home."

I worried about Alicia that afternoon, about Alicia and all the super moms who dedicate themselves to both career and family, focusing their attention intermittently on whichever is making the greater demands at the moment. Tomorrow, or the next day, when Alicia returned there would be a greater challenge in mentoring her because whenever work issues and home issues are so closely intertwined, it is never possible to mentor the work part exclusively. This was like so many mentoring situations I've been in. I've listened to problems involving everything from broken hearts to marital upheavals; I've been involved in the bringing up of children and the care of elder parents. Not part of work, you say? Think again. Nobody lives in a vacuum, and we all bring our challenges to work. That's why mentoring is an art.

The Conflict between Supervising and Mentoring

The situation with Alicia is a good illustration of why supervisors are not the best mentors for their subordinates. At a time like this, the biggest dilemma for a supervisor is whether to consider group performance or the individual first. If I had really seen myself as a supervisor, I might be leaning toward finding a way to keep Alicia at work. She was a workhorse, the kind of employee who is usually replaced by two when she leaves. A few supervisors I have known would have sent work home with her. Others would be satisfied that if she took a couple of days off, she could return to work with a fresh perspective and begin anew at the same pace. Still a third group would maintain a hands-off policy. As her mentor, I wanted her to find the answers that were *right for her*, regardless of the impact on the work. In my years of experience, I have *never* found an indispensable person. The work always gets done, somehow.

Still, I must admit I was feeling pretty guilty when I went home that night because Beth Powell noticed it immediately. We had gone out for Italian food over Beth's protests. "You don't need to take us out. I make a better lasagna than we can get anywhere in town." When I didn't respond immediately, she remarked, "You're not yourself, Rachel. Something at work or is it that boy of yours that is troubling you?"

"I'm sorry I'm not great company tonight," I replied. Then I told them about Alicia. "I feel so responsible," I said, "and I'm really not sure there's anything I can do to help her. I thought if I sent her to PWE she would learn more efficiencies and it would help her, but it hasn't."

"Perhaps being more efficient isn't the problem," said Beth sympathetically. "I know people who get so wrapped up in whatever they are doing, they just can't let go of it."

"Don't look at me," injected Lucien. "I've learned over the years that Beth requires my full attention, and I'd better give it to her—or else."

"Lucky, hush. This is serious. Anyway, Rachel, it was in the cards that when Alicia learned some new ways to do things, she'd double check everything the old way."

"But she wants my help, and I really don't know how I can do that. I've already messed things up," I said, feeling a twinge of guilt mixed with self-pity.

"Don't fret," said Beth. "The jolt Alicia needed was probably administered by the right person and far more effectively than you could do it."

"You mean by Tomás," I said. "That's all well and good, but what happens now?"

"Your job is to be a good 'follower,'" said Lucien.

"So I hide in the underbrush to make sure she can battle her personal 'lion' herself?"

"Exactly," replied Lucien. "And being the wise counselor you are, if Alicia comes to you, the greatest help you can offer is not in supplying answers, but in asking her the right questions."

The next morning I went to see Lily Sheldon. As Human Resources Manager, she was in charge of the employee policies, and although I had been willing to ignore her status in the "wall situation," I knew better than to "tinker" with company policy. I wanted to know what we could offer Alicia, that is, if she decided to stay. The idea of sitting back and watching someone who understood the business and contributed so much walk out the door without considering the options available was unthinkable. At the same time, I recognized she might choose to leave. I felt the age-old conflict between the needs of the individual and my responsibility to the organization. On one hand, I wanted Alicia to do whatever was right for her; on the other I hoped she would decide that was to remain at TYH.

When I described Alicia's quandary, Lily was sympathetic. Unfortunately, most of the options I was considering were not available at To Your Health. People didn't work at home here, and there were no part-time permanent jobs. If Alicia wanted temporary status or a leave of absence, either could definitely be arranged. I should let Lily know. Beyond these options, there was little she could do. However, since the company had been bought by Perry Winkle Enterprises, it was inevitable that policies would change. For now, that was the best she could offer.

Alicia's Dilemma

I didn't think Alicia would be interested in either, but I felt better knowing what the choices were. She returned Friday morning and, breaking with her usual practice of going directly to her office, she stopped by mine. "Is this a good time, Rachel?" she asked, closing the door behind her at my nod.

"I'm glad you're back, Alicia. I was worried about you. Is everything all right?"

"I'm not sure what to do," she said, sinking into one of my guest chairs. I came around my desk and sat in the other. "Tomás and I talked Wednesday night, and he took yesterday off from work. I don't need to tell you, this is serious." I nodded my agreement. "He told me he's been very patient with me because he knows how dedicated I am to my job, but he said I should have known Roberto wasn't doing well in mathematics. Yesterday, we went to the school and met with all his teachers. He hasn't been turning in his homework or doing much in any of his classes. In some classes he is failing; in others, his grades are going down. When we spoke to him last night, he said he couldn't see the blackboard. I'm leaving at ten today to take him to the eye doctor. We think he needs glasses. I hope that's all it is."

"So do I," I responded.

"Tomás asked me who came first, my job or my family. I told him my family. Then he said, I hadn't been acting that way. That really hurt. I offered to quit my job, Rachel, and he said it was up to me. Whether I go or stay, I need to arrange things so I can spend more time with my children. The problem is, I don't know whether I can do my job in fewer hours. I haven't had time to put in the changes from PWE, and the more time I'm away from work, the more backlog I seem to have. With fewer hours I'll never catch up, but if I don't do that, my husband and family suffer. So what should I do?"

At that moment, the tug of war between supervisor and mentor was over for me. Alicia's needs as a person took priority. Like many mentors before me, I had the desire, yes the strong urge, to offer advice. Thank goodness, I didn't give in to it. *I do not have a degree in psychology or family counseling, and I do not believe in practicing without a license.* "What would you like to do?" I asked.

"I don't know. I value your advice, Rachel. What would you do in this situation, if you were me?"

"I wish I could tell you," I said, resisting the desire to share my 'wisdom,' "but what *I* would do isn't important. Everyone is different, and what would be a good answer for me right now at this time of my life might be the worst answer for you at this time in yours. I guess in one way, I would do exactly what you're doing, Alicia. I'd talk to someone and then make my own decision."

"But you've helped me before, and I thought you'd want to," she said, her eyes were filling with tears.

The Power of "Purpose"

"And I'm here to help you think it through right now. So, let me ask you again, what do you really want?"

"I guess I'd like to keep working, if I could do it without neglecting my children."

"So, what you're saying is, your family is more important than your job, right?"

"Is that wrong, Rachel?"

"No, it's right for you, and that's what's important. Remember when we talked about your purpose in terms of your work life? Would you mind stepping back for a few minutes and sharing with me what your life's purpose is?"

"I don't know what you mean by that."

"Well, I'm not talking about purpose in the religious sense. *What I am talking about is what you do in life that brings you the greatest satisfaction, and at the same time, provides the greatest benefit to others.*"

"I still don't think I understand. Do you know what your purpose is?"

"I think so. It's to help others learn to take responsibility for their lives. When I'm doing that, I have an inner sense of wellbeing."

"And you're good at it too."

"Thanks, Alicia. I work at it because I think it's so important. Sometimes I find myself failing when I become overly parental with my nineteen-year-old son, but in the end, that is where I get my greatest satisfaction. Does that help?"

"Yes, but I'm not sure what mine is. Why does it matter right now?"

"I believe *the best chance you have of finding the right answer is to step back from the problem and put things in a broader context.*"

She sighed. "Okay, I guess my purpose is to be a good mother."

I smiled. "That's a start, Alicia, but if that were all, then when your children grew up, you would essentially have no purpose in life. Now that happens to a lot of people who get depressed by the 'empty nest,' but one way to avoid it is to ask yourself what you have to offer, to your family and to the world."

"I think it's that I live up to my commitments. Is that what you mean, Rachel?"

"Partly. Suppose you have to choose between commitments, like the ones you made to your family and your work."

"Then family comes first because they need me."

"Okay, part of your purpose is to live up to your commitments. But not all your commitments are equal, right? So which ones are the most important?"

"That's a hard question. I think the answer is the commitments I make to others."

"What about the commitments you make to yourself?"

"I guess they are even more important, aren't they?"

This was an opportunity I refused to waste. Offering feedback and giving advice are different. I believed this feedback would help Alicia. What she did with it would be up to her. *"Commitments to yourself are more important in my opinion.* It's interesting to me, Alicia, that we are most prone to break our promises to ourselves. We're going to eat better, exercise more, you know what I mean. Then, we continuously make excuses as to why we don't live up to them. I think you're very different from that. You've got a sense of duty that far exceeds that of most people. The problem comes when you make too many commitments and try to do them all."

She was silent for a moment, thinking about this. "You're right, Rachel. From the time I was a little girl, I've always known that I must live up to my commitments. My mom and dad made great sacrifices to send me to college, but most of all they brought me up to be very responsible. My parents worked hard, and I have them to thank for who I am."

Defining Options

"And who you are right this minute is a woman faced with a big question about what she wants to do. What do you see as your options?"

"I guess continue to work or resign."

"Is another to work shorter hours? The question is do you really want to work?"

"I do, if I could handle it and be there for my children too."

"Okay, let's define what *be there for my children* means."

She was thinking out loud now. "It means being home early enough to check on their homework and talk to them about school. It means taking Roberto to get his eyes checked and not worrying about leaving the office. Does that make sense to you?"

"It does, one hundred percent. I have a son, too, Alicia, and I did all those things when he was very young because they were important to me then. Now that he's grown up, my priorities have changed. What time of the day would you have to leave to do what you've described?"

She thought a minute. "Probably by four or four thirty at the latest. But I'm worried that I can't do that and get my job done."

"You get here at seven every day. That's an eight hour day, Alicia. Why not try it for a while and see how it works out? What do you see as the obstacles?"

"Well, I don't have anyone to help me. I think if I could get these new systems put in, I could do it, if Judy could help. I really don't know, Rachel."

"Okay, here's where I come in. Let's get you some temporary support until the new systems are in with the understanding that you are out of here, rain or shine, every day at four thirty. Since you're a person who keeps her commitments, that should be a promise you make to yourself as well as to your family."

"Yes, but who could help me? If I have to train someone..."

"Here's what I'm thinking, Alicia. I'll call PWE and see if they can loan us one of the people you worked with there, say for a week or so. I also think Judy would love to pick up some of the work you are doing. She's been begging for something more to keep her busy, and if you hand off some of the reports, it will be a learning experience for her as well. The hardest part for you might be having confidence in the work of other people, but that's an important step *because nobody functions well without responsibility.* If Judy is to do a good job, she has to feel that it's hers to do. That means your resisting over-managing and re-checking everything."

"I do that, I know, but my mother taught me to look things over—as many times as it takes to get them right."

"If you're going to succeed in this and not drive Judy to distraction, you're going to have to *let go* of some of the rechecking and change the way you work. That isn't going to be easy for you, but it's good practice for parenting too." I decided this would be a good time to emphasize my own struggles to let go. "What I'm learning over time," I said, "is letting go is hard to do but absolutely essential, if you want others to grow. I must admit I'm still working on it with my son Brad, and I'm getting plenty of practice. I keep wanting to mother him back to school, and Paul keeps posting 'danger' signs. Thank goodness I can read them—most of the time."

NOTES TO MENTORING FILE

Counseling on Personal Problems

Don't—unless you have a license that says you're qualified to do it. Neither should you ignore personal issues. There is really no way to separate personal life from work life particularly when one is impacting the other. So, here are the steps you can take:

1. Focus on the *impact* that the issues are having on the individual.

2. Listen and ask thoughtful questions to help the person think through her problems.

3. Ask questions to help the other person clarify the issues.

4. Help the person develop a list of options. Be willing to suggest options.

5. Provide referrals, if needed, to qualified professionals.

CHAPTER 14

Transitions and Changes

You cannot step twice into the same river, for other waters are continually flowing in.

— Heraclitus

The next week was relatively uneventful. Word had trickled back through Judy that the marketing calls on "old" customers had gone well last week and that the new vitamin mini-caps were promising to be "hot." The marketers returned on Monday, off-loaded their sales and expense information to Alicia and holed up in their offices to make the second round of contacts. Between their phone calls, I was able to spend a few minutes with Tom. Justin had done well. He grinned, "I told the kid, I mean Justin, Ms. Rachel, so don't look at me that way—that if he took a few deep breaths and didn't panic, all would be well. Father Tom knows the score. Anyway, he is a natural. Now we're getting ready for the big tour. We're gonna move out of the minors," he said turning back to pick up the phone.

Justin confirmed what Tom had said. "I think I'm getting the hang of it, Rachel. Tom's a good teacher—for an old man." I could see they understood each other. As for me, time to exit stage left.

I dropped by to see Katy. Stuart had worked with her one full day, and he was helpful. Katy seemed self-assured. "It was fun, Rachel," she told me. "I'm ready to go for it on my own." She was leaving for Florida Tuesday. She had already made contacts at Ft. Lauderdale, Miami and Tampa. "They seemed very interested, particularly when I mentioned the mini-gelcaps. I'm not much on those giant size vitamins that feel like you're putting a stone down your throat."

I nodded. "You know the secret of selling is loving the product. If you come back looking too rested, though, I'm going to wonder how the beaches were."

She grinned. "I'll put on my stressed-out look for you, Rachel. Then you'll never guess, because I always have a sun tan." We both laughed.

My last stop was at Stuart's office. He was blasé. Yes, things were fine. No, there was nothing he needed. Had I talked with Elroy about his coming up there? I had, and Elroy was on vacation. If he still wanted to go by Perry Winkle, I could get one of my colleagues to show him around. He didn't and said thanks anyway.

Things had settled down with Alicia. She had been leaving every day by four thirty, and Judy had taken over one report and all the scheduling. For my part, I had called Ira Sharp, Human Resources Manager and my supervisor, who promised to see if he could arrange for Joanne Jackson to spend a week or two in Houston helping Alicia. He thought she would enjoy coming since she had a sister or somebody living here that she visited frequently. He could make no promises, but he would do his best. Besides, the computing manager owed him a favor. He'd sent one of our trainers there to help design a new workshop. He'd call back as soon as he knew, and I was to keep my fingers crossed.

Wednesday, I heard good news from Ira. Joanne Jackson, who had worked with Alicia at Perry Winkle, was at the end of a project and would be here next week. She could spend one week, but that was all. Alicia was thrilled. That night, I called Paul. Did he want to come up here this weekend? He did and finished with an update on Brad. As forecast, our son had quit his pizza job. He was now happily waiting tables at the Rainbow Inn. He and the manager got along well (it had been three days), and he was sure he could move up to assistant manager before long. I sighed, "Same song, second verse."

"Well, maybe," Paul replied, "but remember, he brings the lessons of his previous jobs with him." I hoped so. And there was more. Brad needed some new clothes for this job. The waiters all wore white dress shirts, black slacks and black loafers with tassels. Dress was important because the Rainbow Inn was upscale from his former jobs. Of course, what wasn't! The restaurant supplied the ties.

"You didn't." I said, knowing Paul had come up with more money for Brad's wardrobe.

"I did," he responded. Then, to my sigh, he added, "but I told him it's the last until he goes to school."

"Good," I responded. "We can't afford to keep him working."

What about the apartment? He was still there. "He comes here more often though," Paul reported.

"Really?"

"Yep, we have a washer and dryer without slots."

So now my son had advanced in his career. He was serving catch of the day. I longed to send him back to school, but I knew Paul was right. If he decided to go, he would have to do it

206

because he wanted it. If he went to please us, we would merely bankroll his half-hearted efforts.

My weekend with Paul was a triumph of *negotiation*. I allowed him convince me to let the situation with Brad take its natural course (which I had already decided to do), and he let me persuade him to stop bankrolling Brad (which Paul had already decided to do). When the subject of our son came up, it was discussed for five minutes, then laid to rest for the weekend. Saturday night we went with the Powells to the Houston symphony and then to a late dinner. I was feeling great, but when Paul left on Sunday evening it was raining, and I realized how lonely I was without him. The holidays were coming up, and I began to think about when I would return to Oakville.

Monday morning was one of those beautiful fall days right after a rain when the sky is just a little bluer than before and the air is cooler and fresher. As I drove to work, I was filled with anticipation. The Marketers would be returning today, and although they would be working in their offices, I had noticed how quiet the place was without them, almost like a return to the way it had been when I first arrived. It was their absence that had suddenly awakened me to the level of energy I was finally seeing—a very healthy sign, for which I did not credit myself. Forces of change were at play. Altis was leaving, and although it had not been officially announced, people knew it. Also, PWE had finally shown some credible interest in its acquisition of the vitamin company as evidenced by Elroy's impending visit on Wednesday. I had made up my mind to take advantage of my time with him to talk about going home.

As soon as I settled in for the day and filled my cup with tea, I decided to pay Lily Sheldon a visit. I knew Elroy would want to talk with her, and I decided to give her some advance notice on what I thought his interests might be. While I still thought Lily typical of some Human Resource Managers that I have known, that is, principally an administrator, I had softened my opinion quite a bit when we talked about Alicia's dilemma and

Justin's salary, for she had been helpful and sympathetic. As for Elroy's visit, she was pleased he was coming and said she'd be ready if the questions of pay and benefits were raised. As I left, she told me she appreciated my letting her know, and I gathered her opinion of the leader of the "picture rebellion," had likewise softened.

Early in the afternoon, the pace began to quicken. Joanne arrived from PWE and after a short visit with me was off to make Alicia's life better; the Marketers began emerging from their office cocoons, and Justin came by to tell me he, Katy, Stuart and Tom had been congregating in Tom's office to review their trips. I decided that the level of energy I was seeing and hearing bespoke positive results, and I left everyone to themselves, not wanting to interrupt the flow. Before leaving that evening, I went by Alicia's office to make sure she was gone. She and Joanne had disappeared, leaving a do-not-disturb sign on Alicia's door. I smiled. It looked like all was well.

Tuesday afternoon, a delegation of Tom, Justin, and Katy dropped by. Stuart was working in his office, they told me. I understood. They were excited about the results. Some of the meetings with potential new customers had been just that, but there were orders as well, and the new product was generating interest. Once the advertising campaign started, things would be looking even more positive. For my part, I reminded everyone of Elroy's visit. He had told me he was going to find a few minutes to chat with each person, and I hoped they would all be available Wednesday or Thursday. I really wasn't sure of his schedule. Elroy, as I have said before, is not a man who counts his days out in minutes. While that impetuosity can make him exciting to be around, it is a source of dread for most who try to work his schedule during visits. I wasn't doing it, having been burnt before.

Not unexpectedly, he burst in my office Wednesday morning just after ten. He had arrived at nine and rented a car at the airport, having rejected my offer to meet his plane. "Been to

Houston before. Rotten traffic," he had told me. "No reason for you to be out in it, Rachel. I'll come by to see you after I spend some time with Altis. Don't wait for lunch. I'm taking him to a quiet place— to talk." Goodbye, Altis.

The Fate of TYH

True to his word, Elroy returned slightly after two. Things were moving, he said. They always did when "the bear" was around. "You've done good things here, Rachel," he told me. "I stopped by and visited with Lily Sheldon for a few minutes. I'm going to spend more time with her tomorrow afternoon when I get back from Sugar Land. One thing about it, everyone has noticed what you've accomplished."

"I haven't done that much," I said.

"Don't be too self-effacing," he told me. "I know you. You've certainly stirred the pot. Rachel, I guess you know Altis is leaving. As a matter of fact, he plans to be gone by the end of November. Then, there's going to be a reorganization at the top of TYH."

"So, can you tell me?"

"To Your Health is getting a new President, a fellow named Chris Butler. I don't think you know him. Chris headed up Legend Pharmaceuticals, and they have about fifty health food stores as part of their chain. He's innovative, can turn on a dime, and has vision. We were lucky to get him."

"Well, I've certainly heard of Legend."

"They are a great company. Chris is a leader, and he'll have things humming around here. Just watch him. I've got his word he'll stay on for at least three to four years, time to groom his successor."

"What about the CEO, Elroy? Who's getting that job?"

"That's part of the reorg, Rachel. Since TYH is a subsidiary, and in my division, I've been named CEO. Now, that doesn't represent a radical change for the company or for me. I'll stay in Oakville and continue as Division Vice President, but I'll come down to board meetings. Beyond that, it'll be Chris' baby. He won't be here officially until January 15, but he'll come visiting right after Christmas, and you'll be near the top of the list." My heart sank. I didn't want to be here after Christmas. "One more thing that might interest you. Your friend Charlie Rothstein is destined for greatness. He's put the Sugar Land plant in the black. We're moving him up to Vice President with continuing responsibility for the plant, but we'll be asking him to help us choose his successor."

"That's great," I said. "I don't know anyone more deserving."

The Offer

"Now as for you, my friend," continued Elroy, "how would you like to be Marketing Manager?"

I swallowed hard. I hated to disappoint Elroy. "I'd love it, but I want to go back to Oakville," I said.

"Is that a firm *no*?" he asked. "Would you like to think about it, say for a couple of days? Talk it over with Paul?"

"I don't need to," I responded. "It is a firm *no*. I don't mind being 'on the point' for you any time, but I want to go back to Oakville before Paul starts using my side of the bed for his clothes."

"Sure?"

"Positive."

"I've got a couple of good candidates in mind, but I wanted to give you first crack at it."

"And I appreciate that. When do you plan to fill the spot?"

"December 1st. If you can make it through the month, you'll be permanently home before Christmas. How's that?"

"I smiled. "Just right. Can you tell me who you're going to name?"

"When I know for sure, you'll be the first one I tell."

That was good enough for me. "Do you want to meet the Marketers?"

"Yes," he responded, "but keep your seat. I'll just walk around and introduce myself." He rose. "Got any plans for dinner tonight? I'd like to talk more, after I meet everyone. And you can have your pick where." I didn't have any plans, and so we agreed that we would leave for dinner right after work. Then Elroy could return to his hotel and make some calls, and I could tell Paul the good news.

I saw Elroy once again at the end of the day. He had dropped by to see Lily, and she walked back to my office with him, grinning from ear to ear. Elroy has that effect when he wants to.

"We're going to look at the salary system tomorrow," said Lily. Then in a conspiratorial half-whisper, she added, "It's going to change after... you know what I mean." She smiled at me and winked. I knew. It always feels great to be part of "the club."

Dinner was at The Taste of Texas, one of Houston's better steak places. "That Katy is something else," Elroy said, pausing between bites of a luscious tomato and Roquefort cheese salad. She's a go-getter, isn't she, Rachel?"

"I think she is," I responded.

"She and I talked about her eventually transferring to PWE, and I think that's probably in the cards later on, maybe a year or two down the line. She says she'd probably prefer to stay in Houston or move to a location in one of the larger cities, because of her social life and all. I liked Tom Gaines too. He's happy where he is and I might add a member of your fan club. He says you're a good leader. I told him I knew that. I stopped by and waved at Alicia. She and I met last month, so I didn't spend any time with her. Besides, I noticed Joanne had come to visit."

"Yes, Ira arranged to have her here for a week, and believe me, I'm grateful."

"Justin seems like a nice young man, too. Rachel, he looks too darn young to be married and a father. I think I'm getting old."

"Then I probably shouldn't admit it, but he looks young to me too. Still, I think he's got a lot of natural talent. Charlie Rothstein has his eye on him for a later assignment to the plant."

"Tom Gaines thinks he has potential. So do I. Anyway, Justin credits you with bringing him in to Marketing and helping him get a good start. I think he wants to adopt you. You'll have to go home and tell Brad he's got competition."

"I like him too. I think he's going to be a super salesman. Tom is really helping him. Did Justin mention his concerns about his salary?"

"No, but I did. I told him things were going to change in the near future. He liked that. As a matter of fact, I carried that message to Lily Sheldon. She doesn't like the system either. Says it's a real de-motivator."

"And did you talk to Stuart?"

He nodded. The waiters arrived, removed our salad plates and came back with two sizzling rib eyes. "Rachel, I told him that there were always possibilities at Perry Winkle for those who earned them. I also told him that I trusted you implicitly, and if someone wanted to impress me, he first had to impress you." I was silent. I don't know what I had been hoping, but I felt the situation with Stuart was about to get worse. "Have you decided what you want to do about him yet?" Elroy asked.

"The decision about his future is strictly up to him," I said.

"Then let's leave it that way," he responded.

CHAPTER 15

A Mentoring Moment

No man is angry that feels not himself hurt.

— Francis Bacon

T hursday was a relatively quiet day. Elroy spent the morning in Sugar Land, touring the plant and visiting with Charlie Rothstein, soon-to-be Vice President of TYH. Alicia and Joanne stopped by to tell me how their project was going. I should have been feeling euphoric about being permanently home before Christmas, but I couldn't help feeling anxious about the situation with Stuart. Should I go by his office and see what was going on, or wait? My instincts told me waiting was a better choice, for I didn't know what impact his meeting with Elroy might have had. Stuart had a lot to think about. He had built up expectations about the meeting, and I knew he must have been disappointed. Like most good leaders, Elroy could be painfully straightforward.

I didn't have long to wonder. Friday morning when I arrived, Judy said Stuart had called, and he wanted to see me. I took a few deep breaths. This was not an encounter I was looking forward to.

The Event

"Good morning," I said, mustering a smile, as I entered his office. "You had a successful trip, so I hear. Congratulations."

He was having none of my small talk. "That's beside the point, Rachel, *isn't it*?" he responded. "I suppose by now *your friend* has told you about our meeting."

I refused to be coy. "Yes, he told me."

"It didn't go very well, Ms. Hanson, thanks to your good offices."

"I don't know what you mean," I said.

"I think you do. You made up your mind about me on day one, didn't you? And it wasn't bad enough that you had a personal animosity toward me. You had to poison things with Elroy. Good work. I think you should be proud of your success."

"Wait a minute," I said. I had made up my mind before I went in to Stuart's office that I wouldn't get hooked by his anger. Now I was perilously close to losing my temper, and I knew things never worked out well when I did. "I understand you're angry and disappointed that your meeting with Elroy didn't go as well as you would have wanted it to, but..."

He interrupted me. "Didn't go well? Not hardly. You made sure of that," he repeated.

"I understand that you feel that way, but..."

"Let's don't be innocent about it," he said, interrupting me again. "You made it plain from the beginning that you disliked me."

"I don't think you're being fair. In the first place, Stuart, I've tried to work with you, but you haven't been very receptive. For whatever I've done to make you feel I didn't like you, I'm sorry. What bothers me is that you don't want to take any responsibility for what's happened. You seem to see everything as someone else's fault. Look, I'd like us to talk about the whole situation and clear the air. It's not too late to..."

He stood up. "I think it is too late. Here's what you've been waiting for, Rachel. It's my resignation. Thanks for stopping by. I'm going home now." He got up and walked past me, right out of the office. I was stunned. For a few minutes I just sat there, holding the sealed envelope in my hand. Then I returned to my office and sat in silence, his words echoing in my ears. "Here's what you've been waiting for. Here's what you've been waiting for." Stung by self doubts, I closed the door and cried a few tears. Maybe it was my fault. Maybe it was all for the best. Perhaps Stuart simply faced the truth, and blamed me unfairly. Or did I bear a certain amount of responsibility? We hadn't gotten along from the very beginning. Perhaps I was to blame. Yet, other supervisors had seen him as cynical and disgruntled. Maybe I had been the heir to his dissatisfaction, and the situation with Elroy had sealed his fate. Maybe, maybe, maybe.

I too left early, the envelope unopened in my desk drawer. I sat at home in the quiet of my small apartment. Should I e-mail Elroy? Should I call Paul? Should I knock on the Powell's door? The answer was "none of the above." I wasn't ready to talk about what happened. Instead, I filled the evening hours with soft music and a good book. I fell asleep in my chair and my dreams were troubled.

Saturday I went shopping. The department stores in Houston were brimming over with Christmas merchandise, but I found nothing I wanted. I stopped by the movies and saw a Woody Allen comedy. Somehow today it wasn't funny. I went home and got out my exercise clothes. A walk around Memorial Park would do me good. It helped. That night I called Paul. "What's wrong?" he asked almost immediately. I told him. "It's all for the best, Rachel," he said. "I don't want you blaming yourself. You've said from the very beginning he was bitter and disgruntled."

"I know I did, and he was, but Paul, that doesn't excuse me for being the one who set him off."

"Stop it, Rachel. Don't make yourself the guilty party here. Stuart needs to grow up and recognize the world has changed around him. Pouting like a kid and being sarcastic isn't going to make it any better. Neither will it help if you absorb his guilt for him."

When we hung up, I felt much better. Paul had shaken me out of my self pity and guilt. Stuart was responsible for his own problems. His response to me from the beginning had everything to do with his anger. My reaction to him had been based on how he treated me. That was natural. I slept much better Saturday night. Sunday was uneventful. I went to church that morning, exercised in the afternoon, and watched television until I fell asleep in my living room chair. I woke up, undressed, and took a warm bath before going to bed, but I had trouble falling sleep. When I finally did, my rest was disturbed by a nightmare. I dreamed there was an explosion, and I was running from it. I stumbled over something. It was Stuart, crumpled at my feet. I reached down and offered him my hand, but he turned away from it and I heard him laughing. I started to walk away, when I realized that the disturbing noise I heard was sobbing.

I waited to hear from Stuart Monday, but I didn't. Katy came by the office and asked if I had seen him. I said he was home sick. The envelope still sat in my drawer, but I could not bring myself to open it. I could not shake that awful dream from my mind, or Lucien's words, "*We should not operate based on a philosophy that considers employees disposable.*" Something had to be done.

Aftermath

Tuesday morning I made up my mind to put an end to my vigil. Judy had Stuart's home phone number, and I decided to call him. A woman, whom I assumed to be his wife, answered. I asked to talk to Stuart. "Just a minute," she said. "Do you mind if I ask who's calling?"

"Tell him it's Rachel Hanson from TYH," I responded.

A moment later I heard his voice. "Do you need something, Rachel?" he asked, without a greeting. "You have all the paperwork, don't you?" He sounded subdued.

I asked him if he would come in.

"Is there something *I* need to pick up? If not, Cindy is dressed and says she can handle it."

No, I told him. I wanted to talk with *him*. He agreed saying he could be there in two hours. At ten thirty he walked into my office looking paler than usual. I could see the strain on his face. "This has been tough on you, hasn't it," I said.

"Yes," he responded, looking as if he was close to tears.

"Please sit down for a minute. I'm sorry you're going through a bad period right now."

"Why should you be?" he asked, and then added, "I don't want sympathy, and I don't deserve it. I knew what was happening. *I've no one but myself to blame.*"

I kept silent. He was thinking out loud, not really talking to me, but what he was saying was vitally important.

"I let it all slip away because I was destroyed when Griff left. He said goodbye, shook my hand and I'll never forget what he said: 'Stu, you're on your own now. Run with it.' But I had all that baggage to carry, and I knew I couldn't run with it."

"Baggage?"

"Yes. Griff had put his hand on my head and others had seen it, particularly Altis. When Griff left, it was like I fell into a deep hole, and there was no one left to say that I deserved a chance to pull myself out of it."

"Are you sure you needed that?"

"I thought so then. You told me once I was angry, Rachel. At that moment I probably was, but my strongest feeling was I was just darn irritated by everything and almost everyone, particularly you. I knew the system wasn't fair—but it looked a lot fairer to me when I had a friend in the 'oval office.'"

"I know." I resisted the desire to say more. This was a powerful mentoring moment—for both of us.

"Last night Cindy told me what a jerk I was being," He was looking down, his elbows on his knees, his head in his hands. "She's amazing to have stuck with me through this. It hasn't been easy for her."

"But that's what marriage is about."

"No, Rachel, Cindy isn't my wife, at least not until June. Jane and I divorced two years ago. I guess she couldn't put up with me either." He looked up. "Why did you ask me to come by?"

"Because we have unfinished business." I held up the envelope. "Are you sure you want to do this?"

"It isn't too late?"

"Not if you don't want it to be. I'll be honest with you, Stuart. When you gave it to me, I had a mad desire to run to Lily Sheldon's office and turn it in. But I couldn't, not without giving you a chance to think this through. You were a valuable employee here once. Otherwise Griff wouldn't have done what he did for you. I came in the middle of your story, but I don't want to be responsible for the way it ends. How do you want it to come out?"

He thought a minute. "I'd like to tear that up and start all over again. If I make it on my own, that's fine. If I don't, then I'll look at my options."

"Fair enough," I said standing. We shook hands solemnly, and he smiled at me for the first time in a genuine way.

"I guess I'll go back to work," he said, then turned and walked toward the door.

"Wait a minute, Stu," I said holding out the envelope. "Take this with you."

"You never even opened it," he said incredulously.

"It wasn't mine," I said.

"Thanks, Rachel."

"Good luck," I replied.

CHAPTER 16

Getting Out of the Way

*To leave is to die a little;/It is to die to what one loves./
One leaves behind a little of oneself/At any hour, any
place.*

— Edmond Haraucourt.

I looked at the calendar again. A full week had passed since
Stuart had returned. No one besides the two of us knew
what had occurred, that is, except for Elroy, and I had only
told him after the fact. He had listened but had little to say about
it except that what happened with Stuart was my decision. It
was Wednesday, barely two weeks before Thanksgiving when,
for all intents and purposes, I would be gone for good. *Lead,
follow and get out of the way*, that's what mentors do, Lucien had

told me. As the time neared I realized that *getting out of the way* was going to be much harder than I thought. There was so much going on at TYH, and there were people I had grown fond of in the last few months. I suspected the feeling was mutual. I knew it was time I told the Marketers when I would be leaving, so they wouldn't feel abandoned by still another supervisor, and it was particularly critical that I do it soon because some were taking off for vacation in the next few days. I had been putting things off, waiting (I told myself) for more information about my successor. This morning I had given a vague response when Judy asked me a question about the Christmas party. That was my wake-up call. I was unwilling to keep this company-mandated subterfuge up any longer. It was time to get Elroy's answer to the big question.

The Importance of Transitions

I called. I hated to put him on the spot, I told him, but it was important that some informal announcements be made. Did he know who was going to be Wholesale Marketing Manager and would there also be a supervisor? The new manager would have to decide if a supervisor were needed, he replied, but based on what I had told him, he thought one person could probably handle both jobs. As to who that person would be, Elroy was uncustomarily evasive. "Rachel, I wish I could tell you, but we're waiting for an answer from someone." When would he know for sure? Possibly by Friday. Was it someone who I know? He paused for a minute, and then said, "yes." He agreed the information was important to the group, and he would let me know as soon as he knew. Could I put things out of my mind for a day or two? Yes, I told him, but I hoped to make some kind of an announcement by the end of the week.

He called the next day. "We've got a positive answer, Rachel, but the official announcement won't be out until Wednesday," he said. "No matter. I'm going to tell you who it is, but you're not to give the name out." Would it be possible for me to *describe* the person to the Marketers? Yes, until Wednesday, I could tell the Marketers everything about him but his name. So, who was he? "Are you sitting down, Rachel?" I was. "It's Ira Sharp." Ira is my manager, and I was happy for the Marketing Group, but how I hated to part with him.

"Who is taking his place?" I asked. "Is it someone that I know?"

"Intimately," he said, laughing. "If you're curious, you can always go look in the mirror. We'll talk later. Goodbye, Rachel." I was in shock. Elroy Grant didn't want to give me time to respond. He had decided I needed to take this information in and think about it. But for the moment, there were more important things to think about. How should I tell the group? It was an important question, especially since they had been through so much change. They needed to know that they were in a stable working environment and that the person coming in would be a good leader, as well as a more permanent one. Finally, I decided on a dual approach. First, we would have an information meeting, and I would answer any and all questions. Then I would arrange time with each of them to say a private goodbye.

I needed to move quickly because Justin was leaving early for the holidays. He and Rita were taking their new baby to visit both sets of grandparents. Stuart and Cindy were heading for Florida to visit some friends. That would leave five of us here: Judy, Alicia, Katy, Tom and I. Judy managed to get everyone together for Friday lunch, and I surprised them all with a company-paid celebration at Oscar's, an upscale seafood house just a short walk from the building. Before we left for lunch I told everyone I had a brief announcement. Tom laughed. "You'd better make it short, Rachel. My fried shrimp will be getting cold."

"You need to get off that fried food," said Katy. "Your cholesterol is probably pushing three hundred."

"Not today," responded Tom. "I'm warming up for Thanksgiving dinner." Everyone laughed. I hoped my announcement wouldn't dampen things.

Breaking the News

"I promise to make things short," I said to the group, who had gathered in the reception area outside my office. "There's no easy way for me to say goodbye to you. It's been a little short of three months, and yet I feel very close to you all."

"You're leaving?" asked Alicia, in shocked tones. "I mean now?"

"Well not *right now*," I responded. "I'll be here until the Wednesday before Thanksgiving. I want to visit with each of you individually to say goodbye, but I wanted you to know how great you are and how much of you I'll take with me back to Oakville." I could feel a tightness in my throat. I took a deep breath. "By the way, I know who my replacement is, though I'm not allowed to give his name until next week. Trust me. He's someone you're really going to enjoy working with."

"How long will he be staying?" asked Stuart.

"Good question. It's a permanent assignment. He'll be relocating to Houston with his family."

"Why can't you stay?" asked Katy. "You know us, and you could do this job better than anyone else."

"You're very special to me," I said, "and you make me feel special, but I have another life waiting for me in Oakville, and it's been on hold for a while. Anyway, I promised to make this short. Let's go eat lunch; it's on To Your Health."

"Good work, Rachel. I'll second that," said Tom.

Private Good-byes

So the announcement was made. In the next few days I began my rounds of good-byes. Because he was leaving first, I started with Justin. "You've helped me so much, Rachel, I don't know what I'm going to do without you."

"You'll do very well," I responded. "You've got what it takes."

"Would you mind terribly if I called from time to time, I mean if I have a question about things?"

"No, but I'd sure as heck mind if you didn't," I responded. Justin was not ready for me to "get out of the way," and I had no intention of abandoning him. Before long, I expected he would find other mentors, but for the time being, he could count on me.

Later that day I said goodbye to Stuart. Most of what we had to say to one another had already been said, but he took my outstretched hand and looking into my eyes, said, "We never really got to know each other, Rachel, and I'm sorry for that. But I want to tell you, I'm glad you were here." We wished each other luck and shook hands.

Over the weekend I had dinner with the Powells. They were leaving Monday to spend Thanksgiving with her sister in Biloxi, so this would be the last time we would spend together during my stay in Houston. No matter. There would be no permanent good-byes for us. They had already agreed to a weekend visit to Oakville in late January. They had just bought a patio home in Houston and would be moving out of the complex in March. "As soon as we get settled, you and Paul must come, and you can bring Brad too," Beth had said.

Lucien had laughed. "Brad come here? That'll be the day."

"Lucky, you hush. I want to meet that young man."

"Hopefully, he'll be back in college by then," I replied. "But count on it, Paul and I will be here." I was at work when they left, but when I got home Monday, I was aware that the building was diminished, at least for me, by their absence.

The next week I started my goodbye rounds with Charlie Rothstein. When he heard I was leaving, he invited me to lunch to say goodbye. This time, he insisted that I choose the restaurant. So back we went to Oscar's. "I've heard some news about you, Rachel," said Charlie, as we ate our salads. "Congratulations."

"I'm honored to be having lunch with a new Vice President of TYH," I countered. "As for the manager's job, I haven't yet decided about it. I'm happy doing what I'm doing, and I'm not sure I want something else, even if it's a promotion."

"You've got a lot to offer, Rachel. It's a gift that needs to be shared with as many people as possible."

I promised to think about it. As we parted, I thanked Charlie for all the things he had done for me, for moral support when I first arrived, for having a great sense of humor, for the example he set for me and others, and for showing me the plant in Sugar Land, where I learned that a strong leader can have a positive effect, no matter what the policies and practices are around him. "I'll always carry that message with me," I told him.

"If I give you a hug, would you consider that harassment?" he asked me when we got back to my office.

"No," I said, "but if you don't, I'll definitely complain." So a quick hug and he was gone.

The next person on my list was Katy. "I'm trying not to feel abandoned, Rachel," she told me. "I'm taking this personally. I just don't want you to leave."

"Please keep in touch, Katy. I don't want to lose you either."

"It won't be the same," she said. "You'll have other interests, and you won't have time for me."

I would make time for her, I promised. In turn, she said she valued what I had taught her, but she couldn't promise she wouldn't fall back if I weren't there. I didn't believe her. She would always be bright and aggressive, but she had learned a lot about interpersonal skills, and she was going to be in a training class in two weeks. Another hug. Leaving wasn't easy.

Alicia brought me a gift, a brightly wrapped package of home made brownies. "It's because of you I have the time to bake this," she told me. "I'm out of practice, so if they're horrible, wait 'til I leave before you throw them away." We both laughed. That's what I remember most about our goodbye.

Tom Gaines took Judy and me to lunch. Afterwards, he shook my hand and wished me luck. I asked him to watch over Justin. "I know it's not part of your job," I told him, "but it is part of your legacy."

"You've convinced me of that, Rachel. There's an old adage in sales. Once you've made the sale, you don't want to keep selling."

"I'll remember that," I promised smiling, "and I'll remember you too."

Saying goodbye to Judy was the hardest. She had been so loyal, a quiet but steadying influence on everyone, especially me. I had met her on the first day I was there, and she had represented a sympathetic and kindred spirit from the start. She cried, and I cried. I promised her she would really like Ira. I had already told him what a gem she was, and he was looking forward to working with her.

Two days later, with no more fanfare, I returned to my real life.

CHAPTER 17

Back to the Present

Ah, that a man's reach should exceed his grasp, or
what's a heaven for.

— Robert Browning

T he letter has brought back all these memories. It's
Saturday and I'm rereading it because I want to answer
it immediately. I tend to be a procrastinator when it
comes to writing, but not this time.

Dear Rachel,

I'll bet you're surprised to receive this a couple of years
after your brief stay at TYH. I was with a group of friends
last night having dinner at Oscar's, and we got to talking
about you. Do you remember what things were like when you
came here? Or are you still trying to forget? You called us to-
gether. Remember? I'll bet you weren't exactly thrilled with

our first meeting: one missing, one late, and all of us acting like we were part of a command performance at the home of a spinster aunt.

Rachel, I'd love to have heard your assessments of us when you first got together with the sugar man. He's a great guy, isn't he! He was with us last night at Oscar's and said to tell you hello. Lucky for you, he refused to tell us what you thought after that first meeting. Seriously, I know we must have been a challenge. At the beginning, you really didn't have much credibility with us. We considered you a caretaker, someone sent by Perry Winkle Enterprises to hold the line until fresh replacements could be sent in. The problem was, you refused to act like a caretaker.

When you didn't come back that second Monday, I thought we had run you off. Judy was out that morning, but when she came back she assured us, you were visiting the main office. Aha, I thought, plotting! And you were, I think. We all had a good laugh last night when we talked about how outraged you were over the walls. That turned pretty quickly into action, and we were awed, even if we didn't admit it. Rachel, when you get an idea, it's fun to stand back and watch. You're an artist at making things happen. In fact, I think your specialty must be jostling people out of their complacency.

At first you seemed like a dynamo fixing the place up, worrying about the business, focusing on our petty squabbles, sharing your special brand of wisdom. Then, all of a sudden, you stepped back and said, 'it's all yours. I'm here if you need me.' What could you see that we couldn't? How were you able to pick the right moment? I'm still wondering about that.

I'll bet you're wondering about us too. Well, let me fill you in on the latest news. Katy'll be moving into PWE's Atlanta office next month, but I'm sure you knew that already. She'll have a coordinator's job, so it's a nice step up. Last night she told us she was most excited about seeing you again, (since Atlanta is so close to Oakville), and while I am sure she is looking forward to that, I think it's typical Katy hyperbole.

Tom is still bringing in new customers, and at the same time saying he's going to retire. I don't expect it to happen any time soon, but he keeps talking about his "legacy" so I might be wrong. Justin is doing well. Soon he'll be outpacing all of us. Tom was right. He's a natural. By the way, baby number two is on the way. Justin says you'll be getting an announcement in about three months..

You may have heard that Alicia left about four months ago. She and Tomás are also expecting, and she plans to stay home until this one is in school. About a month ago, Ira created a part time job she can do at home. She's selling products over the internet and, believe it or not, doing quite well. We'll probably never get her back into an office again. We were all panicked when she left until Judy stepped into that spot. You said she was a jewel, and you were right.

Cindy and I have been married over a year now, and while we don't have any plans for a family, not at my age, we do have a pair of yellow labs that keep us busy. So that's almost all the news that's fit to print, except for mine, that is. I've been saving the best for last. Keep this "under your hat" for a couple of weeks; that's when the announcement will be made. In December I'll be moving to Sugar Land as Assistant Plant Manager, reporting to Jena Compton, who took Charlie's job when he became Vice President. And that brings me to what I really want to tell you.

Rachel, I'm not sure you realize what a lasting impression you made on all of us. I know there were times when we seemed to forget the sacrifices you made to come to Houston all alone, far away from your family and friends. And you must have thought we were oblivious to the good things you were doing for us. I confess, I was—at least until just before you left.

So, I'm writing this to say a long overdue thanks from all of us, especially me. You gave me a second chance when I least deserved it. For that, I'll always be grateful.

Stuart

P. S. We all want to hear from you and please include news of Brad.

News of Brad

When I returned from TYH in late November, I had hoped he would be ready to quit his job, move out of the apartment, and return to college. It didn't happen that way. Still enamored of his "new career," he continued waiting tables at the Rainbow Inn. By December, he had customers who asked for him, and he was getting bigger and better tips. In February he became assistant manager. Good move for him, bad news for my plans. While he still didn't like working late, he told Paul and me he wanted to stay there—my twenty-year-old son and someday manager-to-be.

I was worried, but Paul seemed nonchalant about the situation. He understands adolescent boys better than I do. Two weeks into February, Brad made an important discovery. Assistant Managers don't make nearly as much as successful waiters. Then there was a problem with some busboys not showing up for work, and Brad's handling of that crisis was viewed by the manager as heavy-handed to say the least. A performance discussion followed. "I'm not trained for this work, Mom," he confessed. A profound insight for my son. In a week or so, things returned to normal. In fact, Brad was really excited because the manager was being transferred to another city. With youthful optimism, he applied for the job. Needless to say, he was turned down. Too little experience in management and no education, they told him. Two days later, they brought in a new manager, and Brad asked to go back to waiting tables.

In the meantime, Brad's roommate Pete was summoned home, his parents making good on their promise to stop the checks if he didn't raise his grades. We couldn't cut off Brad's funding because by now he was paying his half, but I was sure he couldn't swing the whole rent. To my surprise, he informed us he had spoken with his landlord, Robert Montoya, who had offered him a part time job building sets and doing other manual labor with the little theatre. Montoya was resident director. The pay, together with his job at the Rainbow Inn, would be enough to enable him to stay in his apartment. Strangely enough, it was at that point, early in March, that things began to turn around.

Instead of "hanging out" with his friends, Brad was spending more and more of his free time at the theatre. He ushered, built sets, learned about lighting and before long was attending auditions. He had played the lead in several high school plays, so I wasn't surprised when he landed the role of narrator in "Our Town." In June Brad sprang a major surprise on us, although we should have seen it coming. He was interested in acting and film-making, and he wanted to return to college, at least if our offer was still open. It was.

I thought back. Why hadn't we seen this earlier? It might have helped if we had asked the right questions. I knew of his high school interests and so did Paul. We had supported his extracurricular activities, but when it came to college, we had made some assumptions. Brad needed to get the basics and Westhaven was a good college, even though they had a small drama department. Brad, always a good son, had simply gone along with what we wanted. Maybe I had ignored a silent protest. Yes, I was disappointed too—in me.

Paul told me not to be too hard on myself. Brad had said he wasn't sure of what he wanted—not until lately, that is. What had made him decide to go back to school? It was Robert Montoya, a man who obviously had the *mentoring spirit* that Charlie had described for me. When Brad had expressed an interest in a theatre career, Montoya had said "Go back to school and study in the field." He had even suggested several colleges Brad could attend that have excellent drama and fine arts programs. All of this occurred while I was off at a conference.

"So what now?" I wondered that evening in June when Paul and I discussed Brad's future.

"Subject to our approval, Brad is going to visit all three colleges and see about picking up his studies in the fall. In the meantime, he has accepted Montoya's offer to be his production assistant. It doesn't pay much, but they are doing some work with Public Television in Atlanta, producing a play, and that will give him some exposure to television."

"And what's most important is he'll be going back to school and doing what he really wants to do." But I worried that he might have some problems being admitted. "Last year's scholastic record was mediocre, Paul. I hope he'll get in."

"That's more good news, Rachel. Montoya knows the chairmen of Drama Departments in all three schools he recommended, and that should help. I think our son found himself a mentor."

I was thrilled. Brad had a new level of enthusiasm, and as for me, I decided I'd either wind up going to the Cannes Film Festival or attending some super plays in little theater. Either would be fine. The most important thing was that Brad would be doing something he loved.

Tough Calls

It may come as a surprise that I turned down the Human Resources Manager's job. I thought about it for a few days because it was a wonderful opportunity. In the end, I knew it wasn't for me. I chose instead to continue as an internal consultant and devote my efforts to creating a culture of mentoring at PWE. Elroy was not pleased, and for a short time our relationship was distant. Finally, he came to understand that I was less interested in advancement than in the continuing opportunity to make a difference in other ways.

I had gone to Houston for two reasons: first to see if I could help the Marketers and second to get material for a workshop. While there, I came to understand that *mentoring is more than a workshop, more than a program, more than this year's initiative.* It's an ongoing commitment for every business, large or small, that hopes to survive. The Charlie Rothsteins, Robert Montoyas, and

Elroy Grants believe this and act upon it. They embody the *spirit of mentors*. But the burden cannot be carried by a few. Organizations need to embrace the policies and practices that encourage and reward mentoring. I wanted to help make that happen at Perry Winkle and at To Your Health, and through my story in your company as well. That is why when Elroy tried to convince me to take the manager's job, I told him the story of the starfish. He said, "But Rachel, the starfish that are thrown back into the sea will probably find themselves stranded on the beach with the next tide."

My response was, "Elroy, that is the difference between starfish and people, for when we teach someone what we know, he is forever changed." And so I remained in my consulting job.

Eventually, Elroy forgave me, and several weeks later invited me to lunch to thank me for Houston. I waited until we were almost finished before I brought up something that had been on my mind since my return. "I hope I didn't disappoint you," I told him.

"Disappoint me? What do you mean?"

"Remember when you first asked me to go? You said you wanted to see if I could make the tough calls. I guess I let you down when I asked Stuart to come back."

He smiled and responded. "That depends on how you see 'tough calls.'"

Elroy has a genius for saying the right thing.

BIBLIOGRAPHY

Block, Peter. *The Empowered Manager*. San Francisco: Jossey-Bass Inc, Publishers, 1986.

Heider, John. *The Tao of Leadership*. New York: Bantam Books, 1985.

Mails, Thomas E. *Warriors of the Plains*. Tulsa: Council Oaks Books, 1997.

Spence, Gerry. *How to Argue and Win Every Time*. New York: St. Martin's Press, 1995.

ABOUT THE AUTHOR

Shirley Peddy is author of two business books, *Secrets of the Jungle: Lessons on Survival and Success in Today's Organizations (1996)* and *The Art of Mentoring (1999).* *Secrets* is already selling internationally and is in use in Fortune 500 companies, volunteer organizations, government agencies and educational institutions. An award-winning trainer and training designer, Dr. Peddy has spoken at numerous conferences and has conducted workshops all over the United States and in foreign countries. She has been on radio and television from coast to coast and has been widely quoted in newspaper and magazine articles.

Dr. Peddy is Managing Director of learningconnections, a business consulting firm established in 1994 and based in Corpus Christi, Texas. learningconnections focuses on *mentoring, leadership, communication, coaching* and *teaching the unspoken rules that help people prosper,* even in today's challenging organizations.

Her organizational knowledge is grounded in almost twenty years of experience as an internal consultant and leader of a training organization within Exxon U.S.A. where she worked with a world-wide advisory committee of executives and managers. Her communication background includes being on the faculty of Louisiana State University where she taught honors English and serving as Chairman of the English Department at Dominican College in Houston.

Dr. Peddy's work is (1) to help people achieve power over their lives and satisfaction in their work from having a clear purpose and taking responsibility for their choices and (2) to encourage organizations to help people succeed by rejecting the idea that people are disposable in favor of building a culture that rewards mentoring.

Peddy's educational background includes a B.S. Degree in Education from The University of Texas, an M.A. in English from University of Houston, a Ph.D. from Louisiana State University and professional certification in organizational development from National Training Labs.

Shirley and her husband Red live on Padre Island with their two chihuahuas. They have two daughters: Dana Beard, who lives in Houston and Terri Pitts in Ft. Worth as well as three grandchildren: Rachel, Justin, and Ronnie, whose names you will discover as characters in *The Art of Mentoring*.

Order Form

Please send the following:

I understand that I may return any books or audiotapes for a full refund—for any reason, no questions asked.

Book or Tape (Autographed)	# Copies	Subtotal
The Art of Mentoring @ $21.95 each book	_____	_____
Secrets of the Jungle @ #14.95 each book	_____	_____
Secrets of the Jungle @ $19.95 each audiocassette (270 minutes)	_____	_____
Add 7.875% sales tax anywhere in Texas except Houston; 8.25% in Houston	_____	_____
Shipping rate: $3.00 for first item; $1.00 for each additonal at book rate	_____	_____
Drumbeats subscription—1 year (12 issues) $6.00	_____	_____
TOTAL	_____	_____

Quantity Buyers: Discounts are available. Write or call publisher for information.

Mailing Address:

Name: _____

Address: _____

_____

City _____ State _____ Zip _____

Payment: ❏ Check ❏ Credit Card ____ MasterCard. ____ VISA.

Card Number _____

Name on Card _____ *(please print)*

Expiration Date _____

Signature _____

 Telephone orders: (800) 705-9343 (access 09)

 Website: www.bullionbooks.com
Email: success@bullionbooks

 Postal orders: Bullion Books
9597 Jones Rd., 258
Houston, TX 77065

D r. Peddy's company, learningconnections, provides a full range of consulting and training services for business, government and educational organizations focusing on leadership, team building, careers, coaching and communication.

For information about consulting, workshops, custom on-site programs and seminars and speaking engagements:

learningconnections
14493 S. Padre Island Drive, Ste. A-337
Corpus Christi, TX 78418

(512) 949-8309 phone
(512) 949-8331 fax